HOW TO SUCCEED IN STARTING YOUR OWN BUSINESS

A NO-FAIL PLAN FOR ACHIEVING FINANCIAL FREEDOM

HOW TO FINISH RICH
Written by

SPIROS G. RAFTIS

Bloomington, IN Milton Keynes, UK

authorHOUSE™

AuthorHouse™
1663 Liberty Drive, Suite 200
Bloomington, IN 47403
www.authorhouse.com
Phone: 1-800-839-8640

AuthorHouse™ UK Ltd.
500 Avebury Boulevard
Central Milton Keynes, MK9 2BE
www.authorhouse.co.uk
Phone: 08001974150

First published by AuthorHouse 8/30/2006

ISBN: 1-4259-2691-6 (sc)
ISBN: 1-4259-2692-4 (dj)

Printed in the United States of America
Bloomington, Indiana

This book is printed on acid-free paper.

I have often wondered about the value of a page in a book where the author gives credit to those who helped him develop his written project. I thought the page was a nice gesture. I know now the acknowledgement page defines the realization of the author's humility and gives the author the opportunity to reminisce on the many persons in the author's life that shaped his thinking and success.

I wish to thank my wife, Anastasia, for her unwavering faith in my dream and me and the sacrifices she made to push me on.

I thank my sons, George and Chris, and my daughter, Cynthia, for their contributions to my life and to their growing impact on the legacy of the Raftis family.

This book is also dedicated to the many business associates I have met in my journey.

Many became life-long friends. It includes persons who frustrated me at the time, for they, indeed, taught me humility, how to cope, and how to overcome adversity. I learned to rationalize – learned to put myself in their shoes. They also are my true friends.

They taught me
SUCCESS
SUCCESS

FOREWORD

THE UNITED STATES OF AMERICA GUARANTEES EACH CITIZEN THE RIGHT TO DEVELOP WHATEVER TALENTS, GIFTS, BLESSINGS, OR RESOURCES TO THE BEST OF THEIR ABILITIES.

GOD BLESS AMERICA

OTHER NATIONS OF THE WORLD DO NOT OFFER THESE OPPORTUNITIES.

You are lucky you live in America. The world is yours.

I had a well-paying career and a growing sense of security. My employer even sold me shares of stock in his firm. At age 26, three years out of college, here I was, a successful salesman and part owner of the company. Then out on the street. Fired! WOW!

Where is the justice in this world? Why? What a blow; my career had ended. I slowly picked up the pieces. I decided starting my own business was the only way to prevent this from happening again.

Owning your own business gives you control of your future. The opportunity of earning the maximum return in direct proportion to your abilities. This book is a must-buy guidebook if one plans on starting a business. IT COVERS HOW TO OVERCOME the difficult encounters. It will help in building a successful business.

The confrontations, challenges, and lessons are experiences you will encounter when starting a business.

For example:

GETTING PARTNERS – Outline divorce papers first

BARE ESSENTIALS OF SUBSISTENCE – Why this saying is
    important

LAWYERS, BANKERS – How to deal with them

UNIONS – I was first hit by a union with two employees and then
    again with thirteen

DETERMINATION – How important it is

THIS "NO-FAIL" PLAN GIVES ADVICE FROM THE TRENCHES – SHIRTSLEEVE ADVICE. Even if only one piece of advice shines through, it may be the difference between failure and success.

I asked a friend who had just started a business to review the book. She replied, "Spiros, the part that impressed me was where you said if I fail, I could always go get a job. That thought, going back to a job, made me quit worrying and pay full attention to my dream; running my toy business."

Much is written in this book about willpower, self-confidence, fortitude, character, and catharsis of your hang-ups (Chapter 47). If you start your own business, you will conclude not enough was written.

This story tells of a fourteen-year-old kid mopping floors, and then at age twenty-six, takes five sheets of plywood for an office (Chapter 5) AND BUILDS A MULTI-MILLION-DOLLAR EMPIRE, EMPLOYING OVER 200 PEOPLE. THE STORY OF A MAN WHO HAS DESIGNED AND HOLDS 28 PATENTS FOR VALVES USED ON ENVIRONMENTAL AND STORMWATER APPLICATIONS, AND WHO HAS TRAVELED THE WORLD OVER. A kid who took advantage of the opportunity America offers to everyone.

Enclosed also are sections on Succession Planning and a Start-up Accounting and a Finance Guide.

Regardless if you are one of the readers who is just starting a business or one well in the journey, or perhaps the one planning for succession in a family business, whatever the stage of growth, many sections intend to shake, rattle, and roll the person to a finer appreciation of the birthright America offers to all. This section sells the need for self-confidence, faith, and hope. The messages show what level of success can be achieved by unleashing the power of positive attitude as positive thinking serves to trigger that kind of attitude.

Various chapters contain lessons I learnt working on a plan to achieve the goals of where I wanted to be.

A business morphs into new and different shapes constantly as it struggles to satisfy changing needs, uses, and values of the marketplace. Different problems arise needing not-thought-of-yet solutions. New products to meet customer's needs are required. Management, workforce, sales staff – not even dreamed of in the beginning – create opportunities if only someone thought of these variables as such. The last section ends with what it feels like passing on a successful business as a legacy to family members.

It delves into the troublesome problem of "Succession Planning." John Ward and Craig Arnoff, two professional consultants, developed the excerpt that spells out the main problems and solutions when it comes time to change leadership. Turning over a business to the second generation is like starting a new business. I went through all this, and believe me when I say it was painful. That is why the section was included.

START-UP ACCOUNTING AND FINANCE GUIDE.

What would the do's and don'ts be? This section is a solid, good, and a helpful guide to financing.

This manual is one of those must-buy guidebooks that will, hopefully, lead you to a path in starting a business and stay profitable and successful. Just keep in mind nothing will come with ease, but everything comes to those willing to go after it and stay with it. Success is a masterful recipe consisting of several powerful ingredients such as willpower, fortitude, perseverance, and inner belief in one's self. If you have those ingredients, simply let them grow.

GO FOR IT!

CONTENTS

PART III - THE VALUE

YOU'RE LUCKY – THINKING ABOUT STARTING YOUR OWN BUSINESS

Why this book was written.

I did not write it to prove how tough I am against all the confrontations or inflate my ego. Instead, I wanted to share with others what actually happens when starting a business – the obstacles. Much of this advice, in the form of my experiences, may seem trivial – it is NOT.

I sent pre-published copies of this "How to Succeed in Starting Your Own Business" to several of my friends, ENTREPRENEURS. Their comments were:

> Could not put it down!
>
> I relived my start in business.
>
> Down-to-earth advice.
>
> Terrific! It was like talking to you.

These comments were from self-made multi-millionaires, designers of medical equipment, jewelers, highway contractors, painting contractors, services businessmen, etc.

Many of my friends are immigrants who made it Big Time. They lived through most of the confrontations listed herein; plus they could not speak English. You have a head start – at least you know the language.

They had the need – do you?

CHAPTER 1

Reality of the Business World – Why I Started a Business

I WAS FIRED!

I didn't make this decision to start a business to "get even" after being fired, but I sat back and thought for a long time what should I do next, realizing pouting gets you nowhere. What counts is what do I do now, not what happened.

Obviously, working for yourself seems to be the best move – security. It might take longer, be more painful, but the end results are more permanent.

My life to this point was as follows:

After graduating from college, I went to work for a manufacturer's agent who represented ten different valve companies. Learning details and features about various styles of valves was an education in itself, a gigantic learning challenge. There was a great amount of information my brain had to absorb.

Luckily, I was assigned a virgin, undeveloped sales territory, that gave me the chance to conquer, develop self-confidence, and become a successful industrial salesman. I wasn't following in someone's footsteps. I attacked the job with a pioneer spirit.

Wanting to establish sales in this new sales territory, I worked like a demon. I studied the market and products thoroughly. I came to know what plants were in my territory, where they were located, the principle buyers, and if they were planning to expand. I began to make record sales that not only created substantial profit for my bank account, but also developed my self-confidence, my ego, and my pride.

The owner of the company was impressed with my drive, work ethic, and progress. He informed me that his company had a stock purchase plan, and I was eligible to become a stockholder. This was an excellent opportunity to become an owner (a dream of a lifetime) at such an early age; an opportunity that truly would reward my efforts. I was earning commissions beyond my expectations, so why not become an owner. I was flying high. Nothing could stop me now. I would not stop until I reached the top.

POW! Three years later, the owner called me into his office.

I thought on the way in, *I wonder what size bonus the boss is going to give me?*

He told me my percentage of commission was too high and would have to be reduced. I was receiving sixty percent of the commissions, with the remaining forty percent going to the company. He laid it out for me, "We will have to change your contract and lower the rate to fifty-fifty."

No bonus. I was supposed to take a <u>pay cut</u>.

"Now you know, I told him, that isn't fair. We have a verbal contract, and I'm sure you'd like to do the right thing and keep your word per our contract."

"Things were different when I hired you." His face looked downward.

I hate it when people cannot look me in the eye when speaking directly to me. It gives me the impression that they are either lying or have bad news.

I answered in rebuttal. "No you weren't getting any sales from my territory when I was hired. I built the territory. <u>You</u> should stick to your contract. Why didn't you make the contract fifty-fifty at the time we signed the agreement?"

No answer.

I continued. "Look, you're a smart businessman. Can't we work this out and be fair? I mean, you are making a lot of money just from my sales. You should live up to our agreement, keep your word!" He winced and then ignored me by looking elsewhere.

I pushed on. For as long as I was speaking, I thought, I was in control. "You expect me to be the most knowledgeable, debonair, successful salesman on the road, and the dumbest on payday?"

He looked up at me and smiled. "Spiros, it's great to be single. Think about taking that cut."

I was in a state of shock hearing his proposal. I had assumed he would come to his senses in a few days, realizing my value to the company. I had assumed I could convince him of the errors of his ways by sound logic and reason. I knew I was right. He dismissed me, and I stormed out of his office.

Some time went by with me seething.

I was again called into the owner's office, only to participate in a brief, to-the-point conversation that took all of twenty seconds. He informed me my commission, for the betterment of the company, was <u>definitely</u> to be cut in half!

"That's ridiculous!"

There would be no slicing of <u>my</u> earnings at any time. I should be getting a raise instead. After all, I'm the one of the best salesmen on the staff; I brought in big orders. The company should be enjoying an increase in profit margin on my new customers alone. Why should I give up what is truly mine? I did the legwork and convinced these customers that our corporation would give them the best products, excellent in workmanship, performance, and support service.

I was firm when I answered back, "No, I would not take a commission cut. I am not going to give up what I worked so hard to achieve. I am not going to give up what is rightfully mine."

He was quick in answering back, "You are fired."

It took less than a second for him to say it, "You are fired." Instead of moving up to the top, I was headed out the door to oblivion. What an ungrateful SOB. Didn't I have every right to be angry?

The company then took my territory, divided it between two people, and paid each the fifty-fifty commission split. Here I was 26, a salesman/stockholder/owner being replaced by not one, but two other salesmen, working the territory that I had breathed the first breath of economic life.

Now, at age 26, I was unemployed. I know I wasn't the only person this happened to; however, it was quite a blow to my existence, my rather inflated ego. I found myself somewhat unstable and insecure, believing nothing was permanent in this business world if they can get away with firing a good salesman, a stockholder, and an OWNER!

I pouted for two weeks but did not let resentment get the best of me. Instead, I took time to review my qualifications realizing I had learned a great deal. I was successful in selling industrial products to large corporations and small businesses. That was worth a lot.

Because of my degree in engineering, I learned, understood, and could explain the various technical advantages of any type of valve. I had traveled through all of Western Pennsylvania and West Virginia, knew where plants were located, personnel names, positions, purchasing agents, plant maintenance people, and their managers. I also knew which plants were planning an expansion. I could be a manufacturer representative MYSELF!

Other people must go into business because they were fired, their company relocated, or there was a reduction in labor.

When fired, many individuals must just wonder around with an underlying feeling of resentment.

After several weeks, I awoke to the sudden realization that there really was a bright and positive side to my particular circumstance. Yes, I spoke English well and was a college graduate. I could "cut the mustard" and start a business if I applied myself.

Smart folks find out pouting does not help. They must appraise their plus-minus situation, deciding their course of action.

A friend told me the following story at that time.

Nelson was a shell-shocked World War I veteran who came home from the battlefield and refused to accept a disability pension. He refused such a benefit stating, "I fought as a patriotic citizen of the United States. I love my country, wanted to fight for its freedom, and won't accept a disability check."

Since he was shell-shocked, the government, in an effort to help him financially, gave him a job and worked up a plan with the local officials to convince this veteran his disability check was a paycheck for work. The mayor of the town gave him the job of polishing the cannon and cannonball outside the courthouse. Every time his disability pension contained a raise, he was told the increase was because of his hard work.

Several years later, one afternoon, he went to the mayor's office, throwing down both polish and rag and made a rather unexpected declaration. "I'm downright tired of polishing someone else's cannon

4

and cannonball. I quit, and with the money I've saved, I'll buy a cannon and cannonball and go into business for myself."

If you recently got laid off or fired, take inventory of the skills, knowledge acquired; take advantage of your assets. Nelson did!

In most cases, a person starting a business did not anticipate the move, did not have time to prepare, or plan for it, except in the case of the shell-shocked veteran.

I concluded that the only way to prevent being ripped-off again was to start my own business. I refused to allow myself to be lied and betrayed to again. I kept repeating – I was an owner. My resolve to succeed strengthened each time I remember standing in that office watching someone who controlled my future look elsewhere in the room as he contemplated his next move, which was to fire me. I had turned seething resentment into positive resolve.

Self-pity would only make me a victim. I, too, will go get me a cannon and cannonball and go into business for myself. This is how ridiculous life can be.

CHAPTER 2

No Money

I had very little money saved since I was fired without warning. I did not have time to save, plan, and prepare for a new venture. I was mixed up in my thinking at the beginning.

My first business was to become a manufacturer representative – a business I knew. In looking at companies to sell for, I contacted valve and valve-related manufacturers and eventually landed three companies to represent. It was tough going. It took two months to get my first representation and more than six months to get the first order.

Tough going. After you get a line to sell, you must make two to four sales calls to prove to customers you'll be around. Hopefully, you get an order, which will take two to three weeks to fill, and then thirty days later, the manufacturer gets paid. Thirty days later, the go-go salesman gets his commission check. You know that is what takes fortitude. Getting up every morning making sales calls for six months with no money, just hope and that dream you have.

That started me singing.

Onward Christian Soldier those days.

During this period, I saw an opportunity to manufacture my own valve – "A RUBBER PINCH VALVE." This started me on the quest to becoming a valve manufacturer.

I had sold many styles of valves for four years – had studied features and advantages of many more.

An all-rubber valve intrigued me. All that was available was a manual hand wheel operated all-rubber pinch valve in sizes 1" to 12".

I visualized a market for sizes up to 36" and larger. Also automatic operated rubber pinch valves. I also saw a need for small sizes, 1/4", 1/2", and 3/4" rubber valves. An untapped market.

I knew rubber was an inexpensive substitute for all stainless steel valves.

Let me interrupt this train of thought. I recently attended an Entrepreneurial Work shop. The professor put on the screen a picture of a large block with smaller blocks inside. He asked the class how many blocks do you see? Answers were from six to thirty-two.

We all saw something different.

When starting a business, look for something different. Don't just see six squares, see something more. That's what makes success.

One of the attendees has a flower business. He said he came up with a "Steeler Basket." Out-of-town customers can now send their Pittsburgh business associates a "Steeler Basket" containing local beer, kielbasa, snacks, Steeler buttons, the Terrible Towel, etc.

I did have ambition, self-confidence, and a burning desire. I would design new-style valves that I felt had many features over what was available in the market. I felt so strongly about it that I decided this would be my "new business." I had to work with a bare minimum of essentials with what little money I had. No need for office furniture. No need for a secretary. No need for actual office space. No need for a toilet (more about that later).

A properly displayed catalog for sales purposes was necessary so customers could learn all about the valve I was manufacturing. I knew immediately I needed to get my literature out to clients/ corporations

I realized nothing else was as important as that catalog which would describe my valve and the advantages through pictures and explanatory text.

It was absolutely necessary to sell my products by describing my product in a catalog explaining how my valve worked and would benefit their business, their profit.

A customer in Kingsport, Tennessee, saw my catalog, saw the advantages, read the benefits, and decided he should purchase my valves. This customer assumed, without a doubt in his mind, that I had an office and shop; that I was a manufacturer. I survived during those beginning months all because I spent what little money I had on a great-looking, professional catalog.

7

CHAPTER 3

How I Bought the Land

There is no sure-fire way of starting a business. There just aren't courses of study in college that can guarantee you success or show you each step of the way into a world of immediate profit for your new endeavor. You will not see "Starting a Business 101" in the list of college courses offered.

NOT HAVING MONEY IS A BASIC PROBLEM INVOLVING THOSE WHO HAVE FINALLY DECIDED TO GO AHEAD WITH THEIR DREAMS AND HOPES FOR THE FUTURE BY PLUNGING INTO OWNERSHIP OF THEIR OWN BUSINESS.

Next, I needed a manufacturing plant. I sought out the expertise of a real estate agent. After explaining my situation, he began showing me rental properties in low-rent districts such as old foundries with dirt floors, storefronts, old garages; you name it, he showed it. The prices were all in the same range – between $400.00 to $900.00 per month.

"I can't afford it!" I yelled. "The idea is to make a profit not go in debt! I'd have to spend a fortune fixing those old dumps into what I actually need." Yes, all were definitely out of my price range. After several weeks of shop looking, the real estate agent came up with a possible solution.

"Look, I know you're tight for cash. I have a sixty-acre parcel of undeveloped ground for sale. It's located in the suburbs, and I will sell you an acre. My asking price is $2,000 an acre."

"Why so low?"

"If you buy the property and begin manufacturing, the utility companies will bring up power, water, and gas lines, opening up the property for me.'"

"I get the picture . . . if you sell to me at $2,000 an acre and utilities are set up, you could profit from sales of the remaining acreage?"

"Yup!" He said he would have no problem doubling, even tripling the acreage price for the balance of the land. This is a good location.

"Sold."

Now I said, how about paying for it.

"Well how did you intend to pay in the first place? This isn't going to be a problem, is it? I hope not."

"I had in mind paying $50.00 a month for the first year and after a year $100.00 per month until the property is paid off. You see, this is all the cash I have. Actually, it's all I can afford."

"Raftis, you've got to be kidding, right?"

"No sir, I'm not. I will have to buy concrete blocks and other building supplies. I have to work part-time jobs just to pay for this venture."

"Boy, you are tough – full of drive but not money."

"Hey, you will be saving income tax money since payment of the lot would be over several years, and your capital gains could be spread over several years."

I kept explaining why I needed the land for the next twenty minutes. I emphasized how my lifetime ambition lay in this piece of ground. I would be a lost soul. I talked so long, he succumbed and took the offer. He probably agreed just to shut me up and also to get the ball rolling on his property; it had been for sale for over a year.

A few days later, he accepted my offer. "Congratulations, Spiros, you are now a landowner." He shook my hand as I proudly came to that realization myself.

"That's right, I am fortunate! Someday this property will house a vast company as my business and I grow together."

"I'll just bet you'll make it to success. Good luck."

"Thanks."

It was a warm feeling to suddenly say to myself, "I am a landowner of land for a manufacturing plant." The successful key to this real estate transaction was that I never, at any time, gave in to embarrassment of what little money I had, nor was I afraid to ask for what I needed. I maintained an air of self-confidence and sincerity without any hesitation. You need that attitude to come across with *any* business deal. After all, it was my money, my future, and it will be your sincerity, your money, and your future, too!

I could now proceed to build my office and plant. This would take time, but I was certain of its completion because I had the required drive, strength, attitude, and mental outlook to do it, no matter how long it took.

There are two reasons I wanted to tell you this story. The first is that now looking back on the situation, I am amazed that I actually pulled that whole deal off – no money down, $50.00 a month. Secondly, and more importantly, to point out that America is such a huge country within itself, there is much unsold, low-cost property waiting to be purchased.

Somewhere there is somebody looking to sell, either for tax purposes or other reasons his property. Location of property may vary from suburbia, a rural country area, or perhaps in a desert, but it's available. Closer than you think.

My piece of land was on the parkway between Pittsburgh and the airport.

CHAPTER 4

Five Sheets of Plywood

I had the land. I needed an instant office.

Thus came my five sheets of plywood office. I nailed together four sheets of 3/4" x 4'x8' plywood for the walls and used the fifth sheet as a roof for my office. That is what it took to build my first office. That was all I could afford.

IMPOSSIBLE YOU MIGHT SAY. DO NOT LAUGH; IT WAS FOR REAL!

I cut out a door, attached the front door with cellar door hinges, and installed padlock hardware on the door.

I cut four feet from the fifth sheet for the roof and made a desk with the remaining four feet. Next came the installation of a phone, and I was in business.

Bare essentials of subsistence! A term I carried in my "psyche" for the next sixteen months, also serving as one of my keys to success.

Don't think being fired did not affect me, because it did. The experience was, indeed, extremely traumatic for me because I had worked so hard to obtain those orders, as well as become a part owner. Rejection damages one's ego and is difficult to explain. It took a lot of serious thought before I actually overcame this incident.

The fact of the matter is I did overcome and learned a valuable lesson: IT IS NOT THE EVENTS IN ONE'S LIFE THAT DETERMINES WHO WE ARE, IT IS HOW WE RESPOND TO THOSE EVENTS THAT MAKES US WHO WE REALLY ARE.

I worked out of this four-foot by four-foot by eight-foot-high enclosure for seven months. The only thing that actually got to me was THE LONELINESS.

I felt like a monk praying within his small living quarters in the monastery or a priest waiting to hear confessions in a confessional cubicle. No happy hour, no martini lunches, no companionship for that debonair, industrial salesman who now had his own office with nay an inch for so much as a file cabinet. But, instead, a cardboard box to store papers. The dirt floor was definitely cold, but no time to worry about that. I wore warm stockings and clothes. I did not care about simple, minor adjustments. I had an office now!

Incidentally, <u>I chose to get married to a woman named Anastasia, during this time.</u> <u>She supported me, knew my position (broke)</u>, and was willing to make this journey with me.

My son, to this day, shakes his head in disbelief that this small, four-feet by four-feet building was my office for seven months. I had no toilet facilities except for toilet paper and the woods surrounding my land. I lived like this for seven months but remained cheerful and determined. Are you *really* determined? Do you have self-confidence? Could you do something similar to this if you had to? If your answer is yes, you are ready to begin your own business. Go to Home Depot™ and buy five sheets of plywood, and get started.

BEING POOR GIVES YOU EXTRA STRENGTH AND DETERMINATION.

As I reflect back now, a used office trailer would have solved my problem better. Who knew?

Being determined has its compensation. <u>I was my own boss.</u>

Pittsburgh, Pennsylvania, is a beautiful touch of nature in the summer, but during the winter months, forests appear bland, cold, and almost dead to the view.

The dirt road leading to my "office" was on a twenty-five degree slope. There was very little grass. Rain crested to a multitude of deep mud ruts in the road and around the "office." No matter how hard I tried, this mud would somehow end up all over our home.

Anastasia had her transition – a husband, a successful salesman, a college graduate, and an engineer, no less, coming home with a lunch bucket, mud in the cuffs of his trousers, tracking mud all over the house.

"My goodness, Spiros! You're soaked with mud from head to toe. How can you take it?" She would help me off with my coat, have supper ready, and serve it all with a hot, relaxing cup of tea.

"Sorry about the mud. The weather doesn't want to cooperate . . ."

She quickly interrupted, "Just be careful driving up that dirt road full of ruts. Don't' catch pneumonia."

God bless her patience, cooperation, moral support, and thrift, all without complaint. Anastasia's encouragement and cooperation was and is very much a part of my success story.

When we were first married, we lived for two years in a six-room house. The only furniture was in the kitchen and bedroom. The BARE ESSENTIALS OF SUBSISTENCE even in my married life. My wife experienced the very meaning of that phrase right along with me.

The best tip I can provide at this point in the book is to have a serious one-on-one talk with your spouse or spouse-to-be before deciding to start your own business. You will need his/her support many times over and probably for the duration of your married life.

She/he cannot be buying new dresses/suits. BARE ESSENTIALS OF SUBSISTENCE.

I'm reminded of a person I hired for sales. He loved valves, territory, incentive, and bonus challenge. He quit after two weeks. He said his wife did not want him to stay away from home overnight. Business trips often require several days away from home for meetings.

Make certain your spouse is willing to go along with you on every turn of the road. There will be both good and bad times, more of the bad experiences at the beginning. Getting started takes money and time away from a marriage.

He/she must be willing to help sacrifice time and energy. Think of the future. When profits begin to make an appearance, little by little, it is then that he/she can enjoy the fruits of sacrifices made. It will definitely come.

Do not try with a spouse or live-in who is not willing to make sacrifices or give of their time; you're better off getting a job. Spouse's cooperation is very important when you're starting a business.

CHAPTER 5

Fear of Failure

Mental attitude has a large bearing on success or failure.

Three simple but immensely powerful thoughts guide our every action or inaction from birth: 1) fear of failure, 2) fear of rejection, and 3) fear of punishment. "NO!" The word is the verbal expression we associate with those fears; the trigger that releases a lifetime of collected impressions. "NO" came before we were made to stand in the corner, ordered to bed, or spanked by an angry hand. This hand generally belonged to someone who loved us but also had the strong belief, as did their parents, a child should be seen and not heard, doing only what he/she was told. Our parents and teachers were instructing us to have respect for others (particularly elders), as well as a proper regard for other people's property, as well as your own. It did not exactly teach us self-esteem. That had to come as we became older, or not at all.

"NO!" came before someone turned his or her back on us. "NO," along with our reaction to inner fears, built into the basis for ideas of good, bad, right, or wrong. "NO!" Don't do that; "NO!" Stop that; or "NO!" You'll get burned. "NO!" is leveled in both judgment and punishment. We learn "NO!" Bad boy! And we are rarely taught its opposite – "YES!" Good boy! "YES!" Good girl!

We are graded on levels. In school there is a level of good and bad ranging from A to F, but it only serves to enhance the idea of being judged by others, of seeking approval. The fear of disapproval, the fear of failure, the fear of rejection, the fear of punishment, the fear of hearing, "NO!" all undermine our ability to decide and learn for our success. Fear closes us off from ourselves by turning outward, looking without instead of within for approval, for fulfillment, or for value. We need to form our own self-approval, our own inner self-confidence, thereby enabling us to affirmatively say to ourselves and without hesitation,– "GO FOR IT!"

Hopefully, you are over the "NO!," as well as the "Fear of Failure" syndromes.

Self-confidence is your ONLY divine force. You'd better have it or you're not ready with what it takes for the responsibility of starting your own business. Repeat the "I CAN DO IT" syndrome phrase daily, and actually try to convince yourself to BELIEVE it! You will need this power of positive attitude to avoid and properly deal with any problems, your own hang-ups, and future confrontations.

CHAPTER 6

Go for It

People have asked for my opinion many times regarding going into business for themselves. I generally begin by telling them that if it is something they have always wanted to do, I answer quite quickly, "Go for it! If you don't make it, at least you gave it your best try and got it out of your system."

Look at it this way, when you are on your deathbed, you can say, "I tried and died."

Will Rogers said, "You have to go out on a limb, that is where the fruit is."

If the business venture does not work out for you, you can always get a real (this word might hurt when you say it after failing in your own business) "JOB." Some would say getting a job is a piece of cake. It all depends on whether or not the cake has icing (benefits, good wages, vacations, hospitalization, etc.). Or is getting yourself in a position to enjoy the maximum return for your ability.

There has been a trend in this country the last twenty years for people to start their own business. The reason for this prevailing tendency is that most corporations have become very callous, complex, no longer offering job longevity, lack of recognition for workers' efforts, fewer benefits. Workers are simply sick and tired of working for "Slave Drivers" (CEOs who expect their employees to do a multitude of tasks for two persons and then some, just for a single salary).

I have an acquaintance with a Bachelor's Degree in Business Administration. She had been laid off from a rather well-known steel firm and accepted a new position with a local lumber supply company. As an administrative assistant, she was expected to answer the phones, do the bookkeeping (consisting of accounts payables, accounts receivables, payroll), take dictation, perform other secretarial work, sort the mail, and wait on customers. At the end of one day, she could only wonder when they were going to ask her to scrub and clean the commodes.

Several disappointing attempts later and after working (actually slaving) long hours, she finally took my advice and began a business. It was something she really wanted to do – own and operate a personnel agency – help others secure DECENT employment from legitimate local corporations and small business firms. She carefully tested and went over not only each employee's qualifications and references, but also checked out future employer's complete job descriptions/wages. Her firm is now one of the leading employment agencies in the city.

Start a business. Have you heard of mergers?

Companies that merge tell their employees before that their jobs are safe and secure. When you hear the word MERGE and the phrase, "All will go better for employees," do not believe it. Mergers, from past figures and facts, squeeze many employees out of their jobs. They call it downsizing but really it is the CEO's plan to reduce costs, increase profits (short term), and get more stock options for himself. It is not for the welfare of the employees.

When having a bad day while running your own business, think of the old alternate direction in which you would have to return, you could once again be working for someone else, making you <u>twice</u> as miserable as ever. Just think about that for a while and remember this: When you begin your own business, going backwards is not an option. "Tis forward and onward with nary a failure." Perhaps there will be a wrong decision or two, but these must be treated as mistakes to be corrected. Failures – please do not think this way, not now, not ever.

CHAPTER 7

Know Thyself – Your Hang-Ups

KNOW THYSELF

Up until ninth grade in high school, I had hang-ups accompanied by a negative attitude. My grades were D or below. As a matter of fact, in elementary school through ninth grade, I was known as the class clown. I thought I had everything figured out pertaining to my life. When I dropped out or graduated from high school, whichever came first, I would get a job cleaning buildings or doing maintenance of some sort. If I worked very hard, maybe I'd become a building superintendent.

Then one night a friend of my father's entered my life. He tutored English to Turkish students in Pittsburgh studying metallurgy at the University of Pittsburgh.

He asked to see my report card. He was shocked with my low grades and shouted, "Make something of yourself. You're not like your father, an immigrant with no schooling. You should be ashamed of yourself loafing in school and getting such lousy grades! You live here in Pittsburgh – the largest steel town in the world." He paused, again checking over the grades on my report card. He merely shook his head in a negative manner and told me, "Young men from Turkey come to America to study metallurgy. I teach them English, and these students believe themselves to be the luckiest people on earth. They are studying in America and totally believe in what America has to offer them as students. You live here, was born and raised here. Wise up, young man! You can do much better – go to college." His deep voice echoed like thunder in my ears.

I retorted in a squeamish tone, "Rich kids go to college." He then pounced on me again. "Listen, you can get a summer job and earn enough money for tuition."

Until then, no one ever told me tuition was so low!

I was shocked.

I turned over a new leaf and started studying. It wasn't easy; I had to take catch-up courses in physics, chemistry, math, etc.

I found out it was not only rich kids who attend college but also poor kids. By changing direction and with hard work and perseverance, I went to college and graduated from the University of Pittsburgh with a Metallurgical Engineering degree. This proved to me that any one who really wants to accomplish whatever he/she sets out to do can do it.

I ask that you take time now to review your hang-ups (we all have a few). File them away where they cannot hurt you anymore. Give yourself a complete purging of mind and matter, a catharsis, so to speak.

Plan to make something of yourself.

There is no place to go but forward into the boundaries of your own dream world, which will turn out to be your own very lucrative, profitable business.

Keep that positive attitude and believe "I CAN DO IT," believe even after you reach your ultimate goal, which should be no less than complete success!

Hey Raftis, how about some business tips. They are coming.

You'll find out self-confidence, perseverance, drive, and decisiveness are the biggest factor for success.

SELF-CONFIDENCE
SELF-CONFIDENCE
SELF-CONFIDENCE

CHAPTER 8

Mopping Floors

I am writing these experiences and incidents, not to inflate my ego, but rather to point out that I overcame many adversities and to forewarn you that adversities are coming your way that you must also overcome.

My father was a sexton of our church, which definitely placed me on the bottom of both the economic and social ladders. We were "poor as church mice," as the saying goes.

He had been employed by Bell Telephone as a building superintendent at one of the exchanges. He got laid off in the middle of the depression. The only job he could find was as a sexton of our Church. With a wife and two children, he accepted it and got stuck there.

From the age of twelve to eighteen, I helped him by continuously mopping floors as required (Saturdays and other times after school), for not only the church, but the community center as well. Seemed the only time I got to rest was when it came time to polish various receptacles and serving utensils at the church, being allowed to sit at a large table to enhance the appearance of all brass and silver – religious utensils.

My father paid me one dollar for an entire day's work. This was all he could afford. He needed help, thus enabling him to complete electrical work, painting, plumbing, candle making, and other church chores. He also wanted to teach me all of these trades, so I worked along side him doing plumbing, electric, painting, etc. As I look back now, for he never said this, he really wanted to spend time with me and teach me how to deal with people. I failed to fully appreciate this guidance. Learning people's interaction was more valuable than all the trades he taught me.

How to deal – interact with people.

Later on, I realized this was the greatest benefit of our working together. He shared his words of wisdom. In turn, I now share those words with my children.

There was no time permitted for baseball, basketball, tennis, and bike riding – No playtime at all. Time could not be wasted on such simple things such as sports or fun time. Those particular teen years in my life allotted nothing in the way of fun in athletic participation. They had no meaning or value, serving no purpose in his eyes. It teaches nothing (per my parents' point of view).

To overcome this ordeal, occasionally, I would walk back into the church interior open the door, and cry out LOUD AND CLEAR, "<u>God, cut me a break</u>!" That was my prayer.

At times, I visualized myself at the bottom of a fifty-five-gallon drum, reaching up to the rim with the hope I could pull myself up and out, into something better.

We are all standing in mud; some of us are looking at the stars.

There are many, many people in America who probably can tell you similar stories of early, endured hardships, and visualized themselves curled up in the bottom of a fifty-five-gallon drum. Like myself, they made every effort to overcome each barrier, becoming successful in one way or another, turning a penniless situation towards a more rewarding life.

Make up your mind what you want to do. I never had money for anything, much less enough to begin my own business! But here I am today – a millionaire.

Get rid of self-pity. You do not have to mop floors the rest of your life.

If you're down and out, go for it – pray. God will cut you a break.

CHAPTER 9

The Luck of the Irish

As a teenager, I was brainwashed by friends. I heard it so often that I actually began to believe it. "Spiros, you are Greek, they will never hire you for any big position. You'll be lucky that you can find a laborer's job."

At age 43, I told an Irish friend (incidentally, he was an executive) how tough I had it at that time and how lucky he was to be Irish instead of Greek.

"You have it made because you are Irish and part of the White-Anglo-Saxon-Protestant society."

He replied, "Hey, where in the hell did you grow up? You think Irish people have it easy, huh? Do you know that the English hate the Irish?"

"They do? They are?"

"Yes, and that isn't the half of it! There was the potato famine . . ."

He then recounted all the dastardly deeds done to the Irish. I was brainwashed, narrow-minded only of my struggle as a Greek. I assumed the Irish had it made.

In 1997, I had an opportunity to travel to Ireland, learning all about the potato famine, and how the English kept the Irish down for many years. If "Irish lads" immigrated to America, their families usually never saw them again. They were living in an era wherein they put all their effort struggling just to survive. I was told the farewell party from Ireland to America for these young men was called an "American Funeral Party," because relatives knew they would never see them again.

Get rid of your hang-ups. It does not matter whether you are Jewish, African-American, Polish, Puerto Rican, Filipino, Mexican, Spanish, Italian, German, Asian, or Greek. All had relatives who, at one time or another, have been mistreated and abused in many ways by one group or another.

There will always be someone to blame for holding you back. I cannot make it because my parents are not Anglo-Saxon or divorced, and on and on it goes. When will the blaming stop, no one knows.

The point is, the sport of "blaming" enables a person to become a quitter, to lose focus. Therefore, allowing him or her to climb up on a shelf, to put it bluntly – to quit.

In order to succeed, one must believe in freedom of choice as a chance to reach a goal and achieve what is really wanted. Believe that opportunity is here in America.

The world is only good to the individual as the individual's input makes it. No matter what color, race, or religion. GO FOR IT!

How about that "Luck of the Irish? Italian? African-American? French? Chinese? Vietnamese?" And the so-called luck of all, the other members of humankind. America is a country of all immigrants; each one has a story to tell. Luck or nationality has nothing to do with success?

Darrel Royal, head football coach of the University of Texas during the 70s said, "Luck happens when preparation meets opportunity."

CHAPTER 10

No Toilet

BARE ESSENTIALS OF SUBSISTENCE

Let me go back to the "no-toilet" era in my life. It was a bit comical at times.

I knew nothing about outhouses, never heard anything about how septic tanks worked. I was a city boy definitely use to indoor city plumbing – not outhouses.

I was so focused on getting my business started, I didn't think twice about this need. I knew from my previous sales employment, I needed a catalog, a phone, and at least one sample. That's all I thought about.

Remember, we all have to start somewhere, and when assets are nonexistent or limited, one starts with a dirt floor – take it or leave it. I took it. This was my business, and I was proud of it.

Downside: No water, sewer, or gas lines at that time; I never anticipated this need. All I had was the phone line.

Upside: Lots of trees, bushes, and vegetation. Oh yes, I bought toilet paper; a very important necessity.

I made phone calls from that little "out office."

I could leave my door open in the summertime, feel the warmth of summer, observe the changing colors in the fall, and bear the beginning of cold of winter. I felt I was a part of the forest, sharing the facilities with all the four-legged, living creatures – contributing to nature in one form or another.

It was the best I could afford at that time. I laugh about it now but would dread going through it again. I can only tell myself, "Wow, Spiros. You were determined!"

I began building a cement block plant. Each block cost seventy-five cents and twenty-five cents to lay in place. It was the beginning. Slowly, the roof and walls went up as I accumulated funds to buy the cement blocks.

First Employee

A young man out of a machine trade school applied for a job and became my first employee. He was hired beginning the next day at 8:00 a.m. At 10:00 a.m., he came to my "office" to find out where the toilet was.

I handed him a roll of toilet paper and said, "Out there," while pointing towards the wooded area. "Pick any tree you want."

"You're kidding, aren't you?"

"Nope. I've been doing this for several months now. If you don't like it, go down to the unemployment office and find another place to work."

Surprised and somewhat laughing at the whole conversation, he stayed. He figured if I could handle it, he could too. He and I both found out the real meaning of "cold ass."

Later, people volunteered information about putting in septic tanks. I was a city boy – knew nothing about septic tanks. Since there was no sewer line to the property, I put in a septic tank and installed a toilet in the corner of my cement-block plant. I ran a garden hose for water 300 feet to a house at the bottom of the hill.

I had problems with that setup. The hose froze in the winter. During warm weather, the neighborhood children punched holes in the plastic hose with an ice pick. I guess they had nothing better to do and thought it was fun making my main water line a sprinkler. To them, it was fun. For me, it meant regularly purchasing another 100-foot-length garden hose. Oh well, it was only a temporary situation, right? This situation would change some day.

What little funds I had were spent on phone bills, printing catalogs, postage, a sample valve, etc.

Had enough preaching? Skip a few pages and go to page 43.

CHAPTER 11

Positive Thinking

One day I had self-pity, disgust, and a nasty attitude with plenty of negative thinking. I came across a sign near a church. With such truth and simplicity, it affected my way of thinking. It read:

I FELT BAD BECAUSE I HAD NO SHOES UNTIL I MET A MAN WHO HAD NO FEET.

Look for these types of signs and slogans. There are many of them around. Find one you like; one that motivates you. Develop a positive attitude pertaining to whatever we are confronted with in our short life span on this earth. This means not only in business, but also in our personal lives as well.

A good attitude, accompanied by positive thinking, will definitely help you get along better with family, friends, employees, customers, and business associates.

There is no end to what you can accomplish with positive thinking.

There are several books on "The Power of Positive Thinking." Get one, and not only read it, DIGEST IT.

CHAPTER 12

Onward Christian Soldiers

Your confrontations may be for other reasons than what is described. The reaction and hurt are the same. Someone whacks you in the gut with a two by four. It knocks the wind out of you.

GET UP QUICK.

I found singing: Onward Christian Soldiers.

This would rebuild my morale. I needed some sort of boost. Words to this song follow. Try it. Please also sing it loud and clear while driving for everyone and all angels to hear; it will help you! When you have a down day sing:

> ONWARD CHRISTIAN SOLDIERS
> Onward Christian Soldiers, marching as to war.
> With the cross of Jesus, going on before.
> Christ, the royal Master, leads against the foe;
> Forward to battle His banners go!
>
> *Refrain*
> *Onward Christian Soldiers, marching as to war.*
> *With the cross of Jesus going on before.*
> At the sing of triumph Satan's host doth flee'
> On then, Christian soldiers, on to victory!
> Hell's foundation quivers at the shout of praise;
> Brothers lift your voices, loud your anthems raise.

I never memorized it all. The first two stanzas picked me up enough.

Turn up the corner of this page to easily find it during an emergency.

CHAPTER 13

Metal Buildings

Metal buildings are less expensive in America than in any other country in the world. As the song goes, "if you can make it in New York, you can make it anywhere." If you make it in America, you <u>can</u> make it anywhere!

You have a golden opportunity being an American. Land costs less in the United States (unlike England and crowded Europe); building permits are less difficult to obtain (unlike in India or Thailand).

Yes, metal buildings are less expensive than in any other country in the world.

Remember, America is always on your side. You can make it here. Where else can you begin a business with absolutely nothing? Pause for a moment and think. You could have been born in Russia, South America, or Europe. Where else can you secure land at a reasonable price? Where else can you borrow money from banks, from the government to start a business?

The above remarks have real depth to them. Businessmen and women from Europe and Asia expressed serious emotion in telling me exactly how fortunate I really was to live and own a business in this country. These friends could not build a plant in Europe because building and land costs are very high. Europe is crowded.

I visited a valve manufacturer in England. He said his business was going well, and he needed more space. His shop was in a residential area, which is quite common in England. He related that before he could move to a larger plant building, he would, by law, have to find another employer to buy or rent his building and provide work for his employees. It's not unusual to line up three or four manufacturers to enable a move to a larger plant.

Metal buildings in the USA, as compared to England, are inexpensive because competition brought the price down. Land out in our vast country, "out yonder" so to speak, is relatively reasonable in price. You will have help from local municipalities regarding zoning laws. They generally grant a variance. Building permits are granted easier since property tax money and jobs will be forthcoming. There may be some resistance, but you will overcome. I had it rough for the first ten years because I could only afford a twenty-foot by thirty-foot expansion (Bare Essentials). I had to go through the process of applying for a building permit ten times. One time it took too long. I poured a concrete floor and machined valves outside (see picture in Chapter 14.).

Whatever it takes, we do. After all, WE/YOU are fortunate . . . we live in AMERICA!

God Bless America . . . .

CHAPTER 14

You Think You Have It Tough

This picture hangs in my office.

At the time this picture was taken, I could not get a building permit. Therefore, we placed a boring mill on a concrete pad and machined our valves outside (note the snowflakes – they are real). We needed this boring mill for very large-sized valves.

Six months later, I got my building permit. Again my dream came true!

CHAPTER 15

Theory of Relativity

A hobo is somewhat of an entrepreneur, a vagrant, a migratory worker, and a person who hops trains. This hazardous transportation, hopefully, would transport a hobo to some new, exciting places for work. Maybe a small town in which to escape from reality, or a city in which one could find employment.

There are various hobo descriptions.

My father, who had just come from the old country, could not find employment in Springfield, Massachusetts; Pittsburgh, Pennsylvania; or Richmond, Virginia. He hopped a freight train, traveled to Iowa, obtained a job breaking rocks in a stone quarry. You could not label him a hobo or bum, but instead, an "entrepreneur."

He became very good in hopping trains. He was so good, he eventually got himself a job as a brakeman. What is a brakeman? Before **Westinghouse Air Brakes**, a brakeman would hop from one freight car to another turning manual brakes to put the brake on the wheels of the train going downhill and unwinding the brakes while going uphill. This is what my dad did all day for quite a number of years.

The name "hobo" came from the migratory worker – a person who hopped trains with a hoe and went from farm to farm to do seasonal work. A Hoe Bo – a Hobo.

Here is my theory of relativity. Are you a hobo or entrepreneur?

CHAPTER 16

My Childhood Business Experience

A PENNY

At age fourteen, I had a paper route. One of my customers had a twenty-four-cent newspaper bill and paid me a quarter. I did not have a penny change, so the man told me to go and get change and come back. I walked eight blocks to get his lousy penny change. This was an isolated incident; an experience I will never forget.

Another one of my customers turned out the light bulb in the hall before handing me my change, which included a button, the size of a dime in substitution of a real dime.

I gave up this paper route because my shoes developed holes faster than I could earn money to repair them.

Start a worthwhile business – pass up the newspaper route.

You use your own judgment as to what you are actually happy doing within your lifetime. Why mop floors? Why deliver papers? Why wait on tables? Why sell papers? Is there nothing better for you to do?

Look for a career that you love and one where you learn.

Let's put it this way. I never quite made it to the Old Newspaper Boys Club, but I made it in the business world.

CHAPTER 17

Be a Survivor

During the first year, approximately eighty percent of all businesses fail. Of these survivors, twenty-five percent will fail during the next five years.

Why do the first eighty percent fail? They run out of money the first year keeping the business going, with no funds left over to eat, much less take care of the family.

Many of them will say, "If I could have stuck it out one year, I would have made it."

Before you start your business, figure out how much money you need to eat for one year.

They did not know about BARE ESSENTIALS OF SUBSISTENCE.

The next big failure is some thirty-five years later when the founder runs out of steam and did not have the patience to teach sons, daughters, or relatives how to run the business while it was growing.

The failure statistics listed above are very true. Women have the same failure rate.

CHAPTER 18

Bare Essentials of Subsistence

FEED family and self for the first year.
Make this powerful commitment to yourself.
Get only the Bare Essentials of Subsistence.

Bare Essentials of Subsistence
Bare Essentials of Subsistence
Bare Essentials of Subsistence
Bare Essentials of Subsistence
Bare Essentials of Subsistence
Bare Essentials of Subsistence
Bare Essentials of Subsistence
Bare Essentials of Subsistence
Bare Essentials of Subsistence
Bare Essentials of Subsistence
Bare Essentials of Subsistence
Bare Essentials of Subsistence
Bare Essentials of Subsistence
Bare Essentials of Subsistence
Bare Essentials of Subsistence
Bare Essentials of Subsistence

For example, if you decide to start a business selling gourmet cookies or a catering business, start the business in your kitchen; make deliveries with your car. As it expands, rent a clean garage. Buy a "Bakers" oven.

Have money left to eat.

Have money for promotions (during holidays).

No worries – no doubts – your efforts went into making BETTER COOKIES.

QUITE A FEW WOMEN BECAME MULTIMILLIONAIRES WITH GOURMET FOOD SPECIALITIES.

CHAPTER 19

Business Decisions

LIST YOUR BARE ESSENTIALS OF SUBSISTENCE in order of importance and then price them.

This is my partial list

1. Food and Lodging (I lived at home)
2. Catalogs
3. Stationery
4. Telephone – Computer
5. New Product Announcement
6. Drawings to Scale of Product
7. Automobile Expense
8. Patterns for Foundries
9. Castings
10. Toilet Paper
11. Garden Hose
12. I do Not Want to Get Involved with Partners
13. Buy Used Desk, Chairs, typewriter

CHAPTER 20

My First Million

The first million in sales came after eleven years. If it takes you that long, you are a survivor.

You've lived well on the way and did what you really <u>wanted</u> to do. Some people say, "Spiros, you are a lucky man. You have a valve business that sells worldwide."

Yep! I made it. Climbing the ladder for eleven years to success after starting with only a telephone, desk, chair, and FIVE SHEETS OF PLYWOOD.

GET ON THE BANDWAGON – START YOUR OWN BUSINESS.

It is fun and a challenge – "the Road to Success."

The first million is the hardest!

CHAPTER 21

What Is Success?

What is success? There probably are several different meanings for those who are lucky enough to have found it. In my opinion, success is OVERCOMING ONE'S ENVIRONMENT. This could mean if you are born in a low-income family bracket, not only income-wise or because of where you live, your mindset is low income as well. "No outlook for the future," rules your mind like a virus worming its way through the hard drive of a computer.

Hang-ups that must be overcome.

It could be you hate someone so you spend idle time reviewing what he did and justifying why you hate that person instead of looking at your own progress.

Your failure could be the people around you giving you bad advise or telling you your right; I don't blame you.

Success is overcoming your environment and getting rid of the hang-ups you developed and are carrying on your shoulders.

Overcoming our environment – relatives and friends tend to pass along many causes for some of our hang-ups. This environment could be mediocre friends within our own circle. Therefore, our perception is mediocre. You believe everyone is in this environment. You see life through the same point of view as those who travel with you in the same orbit. You were never exposed to a winning environment.

I love my parents – good – honest – sincere people who, as immigrants, came to the United States with nothing more than a grade-school education, accompanied by a greater will, the opportunity to earn a decent living, and raise their family.

PRIMARILY FOR A BETTER OPPORTUNITY. THEY BOTH WERE WINNERS.

Both my father and mother taught me the true meaning of opportunity and freedom.

When an individual approaches a later age, he/she then really begins to reflect back, to see the bigger world; the way it should have been seen earlier. This is the time you realize nobody lit a candle to guide you.

It takes many years to become aware of the mediocre circle you live in. It may be a domineering mother you must overcome. There are many other forces that pulled you or held you down. Parents that lived during the depression, for example, pass on fear of insecurity to their children.

Have to shake it off.

I have a friend, a successful executive of a large corporation, who confessed he <u>never</u> went into his own business because the fear of a depression was instilled in him by his father's strife during the depression.

The probability of an immigrant child growing up to adulthood with hang-ups is more prevalent because there are definitely no role models within their household.

If you are a member of a minority group in the United States, the probability of suffering hang-ups definitely increases.

Find a role model.

Secretary of State Colin L. Powell apparently shed his hang-ups; he found role models. He is now a role model.

Suppose you are from a farmer household where the father preaches, "You don't' need no book learning. All you need to know is farming. Farming is your whole life." Any books brought into the house were generally thrown into the fireplace. Sons during that era were definitely brainwashed, believing there was only one occupation in life – farming – whatever <u>his</u> father learned from <u>his</u> father and so on. How lucky his siblings are to inherit a farm.

There is nothing more said regarding the subject of a boy's abilities or career. He was prohibited from having any brainpower.

Thank God things have changed. There still are some fathers, who like the early settlers, refuse to allow their sons to follow any occupation other than the family tradition.

Daughters were no different in that they were told to cook, sew, make candles, get married at an early age, have babies (boy babies, so they could work on the farm), do the canning, clean house, help with whatever their man wanted, and Lord knows how much more.

38

Nevertheless, there were no chances here for girls. Male and female roles had been firmly set. You did what you were told to do within your circle.

Ignorance may have been bliss back then, but not today. We have come out of this environment partially, but it is up to you to go the rest of the way. During this day and age, there are many opportunities out there being offered to young people who are willing to "go for it."

You do not have to listen to anyone when you reach college age (generally eighteen). Work if you must, get a loan, get a scholarship if you can. If your father is stubborn and wants you to do one thing, and you prefer another, do not please your father. Unhappiness will follow you in a profession in which you will not be happy.

It is you who must reach for what you believe in, what you <u>really</u> want to do, and not choose it because it may sound good to others, but choose it because it is what you <u>really</u> want.

My parents were from Greece. I later realized some of their friends, mentally, were extinct volcanoes, people relating to stories about the "Glory of Greece" back in 200 BC, the Parthenon – their magnificent heritage. They came to America to seek gold, and many found glorification only in reminiscing about their homeland's past. That they were descended from "good stock" dating back to the "Golden Ages of Greece."

That did not get me good grades – hard work, studying, and a goal were needed to get me good grades and where I was going.

You have got to be mentally prepared for challenges of a new business and need a lot of self-confidence. That is why I am relating my problems throughout this book. Samuel Johnson, a great thinker of the past, said, "Self-confidence is the first requisite to great undertakings."

Beware of hang-ups.

THINK SUCCESS!

The previous section can be summarized as follows:

One: There is a need to know what one really wants to do with the skills, education, resources, and business concept he or she has to start the journey.

Two: One needs to know that Bare Essentials of Subsistence requires sacrifice, so you can last a year in the new business.

Three: Self-confidence and the need to know that staying focused on the goal (what one really wants) means eliminating hang-ups and distractions.

Before beginning the next section titled THE USE, think abut the direction you want to go by answering the most important question:

"What do I really want?"

The lessons in the following chapters are lessons I learned the hard way, but not necessarily through the method of trial and error. I expect to falter, make mistakes, and even fail sometimes. But I do not plan to.

If I stay focused on making THE RED VALVE COMPANY competitive in the marketplace by providing the best marketing campaign of product, materials, workmanship, and service support – all provided within a competitive price – I know I will succeed.

Someone told me as long as you make the right decisions 51% of the time, you'll make out.

If you start off a business with very little cash, you have to do much better. Fifty-one percent won't do it. For example, buying used equipment when you start, not new.

What helps you if you can't afford something is to find a less expensive route. Starting even with stationery – I found a quality printer of stationary in Chicago at half the price.

You too can shop around.

Part II

Confrontations

Suggestions

How to Handle Various Confrontations – They Are Mostly Unexpected

CHAPTER 22

My First Piece of Production Equipment

JUNKYARD EQUIPMENT

I went to the junkyard to see if I could get someone's discarded equipment. Fortunately, I found a medium sized lathe without an electric motor (which was extra).

I offered the junkyard owner $75.00. He bellowed back at me, "Weight of material as scrap is worth more than that."

I replied, "Ah come on. I really need that lathe. Give me a break. I just started a new business. Could you refuse to sell me the lathe, which I need to make a living? I'm broke, $75.00 is all I have."

"If you're that hard up and really need this lathe, then take it."

I talked him into delivering, saying my shop is a half-mile away. He agreed to use his dump truck as long as I took full responsibility in case it cracked when it was dumped on the ground.

Getting it to run was another problem since it was belt driven. I also bought a drill press from Sears and Roebuck™ and was now able to do a little machining. This started me on the manufacturing side of the business. I was a manufacturer.

Today, I own five CNC machines ($900,000.00 each). That $75.00 junkyard lathe started it all.

People ask me, "What do you manufacture?" I manufacture a valve that is basically a rubber hose that pinches close. It is made in sizes 1/8" to 120" diameter. Smaller valves are used on controlling slurries in manufacturing plants; larger valves are used on storm water lines. These valves are called Pinch Valves. For more information on Red Valve Company's pinch valves, go to the Internet. The large valves are so large; people can walk through them. The valve can be closed with a hand wheel, an air cylinder, or an electric motor in all of the above sizes.

Many variations are designed to customer's needs. A customer's need also was instrumental later in our designing and manufacturing an all-rubber check valve that became our best seller.

Because a rubber hose is full round with no pockets (for food decay), it is ideal for food applications. Pinch valves uses also include mining slurries, sewage, chemicals, sludge, flour, and sugar. All hard-to-handle materials that will plug a conventional valve.

I got started in pinch valves fifty years ago after I saw a version of a manual-operated pinch valve made in smaller sizes. The possibilities of its uses intrigued me. Since I had spent the previous five years selling seven different styles of valves to industries, I saw the distinct advantage of a "Pinch Valve," and rather than procrastinate, I DID IT.

I saw the potential of closing this rubber hose manually, with air and electric. I visualized the need for large sizes starting at 12" and over. I was CONFIDENT in making it as a manufacturer because all seven of the different-styled valves I sold before were of little-known companies that made it big.

How many people see similar needs and sit on them – DO NOTHING.

I REACHED BACK FOR POSITIVE REASONS TO SUCCEED.

I REACHED BACK FOR POSITIVE MOTIVATION.

I HAD CONFIDENCE IT WOULD BE A WINNER.

CHAPTER 23

Advertise

"DOING BUSINESS WITHOUT ADVERTISING IS LIKE WINKING AT A GIRL IN THE DARK. YOU KNOW WHAT YOU ARE DOING, BUT SHE DOESN'T."

In order to be successful, I had to let industrial plant operators know that I was manufacturing a new-style valve for hard-to-handle liquids and powders. Even with mousetraps, people must know you are manufacturing the best, most unique mousetrap with many advantages.

I had little money for advertising.

I knew that Industrial trade business magazines inform readers in their "New Products" section about the latest innovations. My best course of action at the beginning, therefore, was to spend what little funds I had on photographs, literature for new product releases, and promotional activities rather than purchase machinery, office equipment, or services of a staff.

CREATE A NEED FIRST.

I repeat this over and over again. One of the main reasons for failure of small businesses is depletion of cash flow, which means cash spent on machinery, desks, and computers. One actually runs out of funds, not necessarily because they didn't' have enough to begin with, but because what little cash they possessed was not spent wisely.

To get results and clientele to make a successful business – ADVERTISE. I let people know what type of business I operated and what I was offering for sales. Advertise in newspapers, radio commercials, and trade magazines. The word of your new product and enterprise must get out to the business world.

I designed a size 3" valve on my kitchen table and then made a sample, which I photographed galore. I forwarded these photos with an announcement to editors of New Product Releases.

News releases became my main effort.

I created the need. Inquiries soon began coming in from all over the United States, from both users and industrial distributors. I then gave drawings of other valve sizes to pattern makers (because I created a market), bought the castings, and still 'farmed out" the machining of the valves. I didn't need lathes. I needed advertising and orders.

Whatever cash I had left was spent printing a catalog, traveling, and expounding the features and advantages of my valve, which I designed, patented, and was unique enough to develop a market. As more literature went out, quotation requests for pricing began to cross my desk. What was even more important was getting calls from manufacturer representatives and industrial distributors across the country wanting to sell my valves. I needed sales representatives who could sell the need, use, and value of my product.

FREE PRODUCT releases paid off. I spent money on catalogs, not on elaborate manufacturing facilities.

My office, **FIVE SHEETS OF PLYWOOD**, was sufficient.

Bare Essentials of Subsistence.

Spend money wisely. First things first!

CHAPTER 24

My Office Facilities

HORNET'S NEST:

I had my office, land, and the beginnings of a factory.

One would say I had it all.

This is all I could afford at this point in time. It served the purpose.

What little money I had, I REPEAT, was put into printing catalogs for customers.

My market was directed to industrial users nationwide.

No customer would be visiting my general office(s), so "image" was not one of my priorities.

One of the hilarious happenings I recall in my five-sheets-of-plywood office was the day a hornet came in while I was on the phone with a client. The only "hornet weapon" handy was a shovel I used to dig the foundation. I asked the customer on the other end to hold on for just a moment and proceeded to kill the hornet with the shovel – Bang, Bang! Thump, Thump! – not realizing the resounding noise this made in a four-foot by four-foot plywood cubicle.

"Hello? Hello Spiros? What's happening?"

"It's alright now," I said. I was a little out of breath. Swatting a hornet in a cubicle certainly was not an easy task. A fellow could certainly get bit many times over.

"Why are you panting? Did something happen? It sounded as though the building was caving in."

"No, I'm okay. A hornet just buzzed his way into my office. I had to get rid of it."

"Did you get bit?"

"No sir. Not even close. I killed him with a special tool I have here in the office."

"Good, good. What kind of tool is it?"

"Kind of a large metal flyswatter." He said it sounded like the building collapsed.

"Oh. Well, let's get back to business."

He hadn't a clue that I really meant "my plywood cubical" when I referred to my office.

The other reflection I remember vividly was reminiscing on my previous life on the road for five years as a salesman meeting people, eating lunch at great restaurants, enjoying Old Fashions and Martinis for lunch. This I referred to as THE GOOD LIFE.

Now here I sit, all by my lonesome, on top of a steep hill, gazing at my acre of land as I wait for the phone to ring in reply to my new product releases in industrial magazines.

I also had the feeling all I needed was a monk's robe. I certainly spent a lot of time in my tiny little area, no traffic outside, alone, like a monk.

I was driven, assured that I would make it in the valve manufacturing business. My one-track mind enthusiasm must have showed. A friend stopped by at the time, and after listening to me said, "Spiros, when you were born, the doctor, rather than slap you on your ass, took an Armours' meat stamp that said Valve Manufacturer and stamped you." Incidentally, I never forgot his quirk. I guess it showed.

I had very little money. My dad could not help me, so I got along with the BARE ESSENTIALS OF SUBSISTENCE.

CHAPTER 25

Hiring Employees

Allow me to skip up a few years and talk about hiring employees.

My first employee was a high-school boy out of trade school. He machined, assembled, and tested the few valve orders I got in the beginning.

I was now over a full year in my new business. I had to get out on the road and visit customers. Employee number two was a woman executive whom I trained to "hold the fort." Initially, she handled the day-to-day problems. I spent a lot of hours later training her the technical aspects of our products, to answer at least most of the questions from customers phoning in.

During my second year, I hired a second "machinist from a trade school. Both had no experience. They needed training; this took a lot of my time. This was their first job.

There were now two men in the shop, since sales began to pick up. What a traumatic experience those first two years were. Going on the road for one week and then rushing back to supervise the manufacturing of the valves.

I wore a cool-dude hat, remained suave, dressed like a professional salesperson, as well as being the knowledgeable conversationalist on the road, explaining engineering features in a convincing manner. I maintained all the attributes of a professional salesperson and uppermost, being a congenial, friendly guy – helpful – cool.

The following week back at the shop, direct opposite personality – crack the whip.

My next step was to hire a valve design engineer as the business continued to grow, and customers needed variations, new designs.

A valve designer, complete with a Professional Engineer certificate, applied for the job. He had six years' design experience with a well-known national valve company. I questioned him about his last job, and he informed me he was let go.

"Why?"

"Because I love hunting. I applied for a hunting license in Wyoming for elk and bighorn sheep. Licenses are raffled in Wyoming. You purchase a *hunting license raffle ticket*. If they pull your license in the raffle, you get to go hunting. Otherwise, they refund your money. Well, I won, and I went to ask my boss for time off."

"Then what?"

"He stated that if I had vacation time left, I could go. If not, well . . . . that's why I'm applying for this job. I'm here because I went hunting anyway."

I thought, *this guy was a bit different. He is definitely not the conventional type of employee. He is independent, makes up his own mind. I liked that.*

I offered him a job and explained that I couldn't afford a large-base engineering pay but could offer him an attractive incentive. Five percent override on all orders from sewage treatment plants nationwide. He stated that was an unbelievable incentive.

"When can you start?" I asked.

"Well, I really wanted first to go hunting and fishing for at least four more months."

"How can you afford to take this much time off work? Didn't you say you are married and have three children?"

"Yes, however, I decided several years ago most bosses are bastards. I decided to save one year's salary just in case I didn't want to work for some bastard."

This is a real incident.

Wow! Here is a guy with three kids and has one year's salary in the bank. He sounds almost unbelievable. That alone is a reason to hire him.

I actually found myself half apologizing for the pressure I was putting on him to start in two weeks.

Well, two weeks later he called. "Tell you what. I'll begin work for you right away. I cannot turn down an incentive offer like that."

"Sounds good to me. Look forward to working with you." He seemed happy enough to show up in two weeks, which he did.

He had confidence in his ability and took the job.

He became a big asset to the business by designing and redesigning products, making presentations to consulting engineers, developing a slide cassette presentation, building sales to the sewage market. He made money, not only for himself, but for my company as well, and spent time working extra hours from his home. Talented people often work harder than what is required. We worked as a team; I learned valve design during this period.

When starting a new business, offer a talented employee an incentive, because a talented person knows his ability and makes you money.

A small business can use a person with a mind of his own who does not fit within a normal corporate structure. A person who forces someone to take notice of him during the interview, someone who looks at the world in quite a different way, often a progressive way, a sincere commitment towards his work.

This man was an asset to my newly formed business, and I repaid him with honesty, trust, and money.

All businesses become successful if they hire talented personnel. The success of a restaurant, for example, depends on the exceptional talent of the COOK.

CHAPTER 26

Business Decisions
Update the list of needs.

List your initial decision.
I have a good product.
I don't want to get involved with partners.
I spend money only on what I need to achieve my objective.
BARE ESSENTIALS OF SUBSISTENCE – I need money to
    eat the first year.
Catalogs.
Stationery.
Phone.
New Product Announcement.
Patterns for Foundries.
Castings.
Septic Tank.
Automobile Expenses.
Customer lunches.

CHAPTER 27

Ask for Advice

Don't be afraid to ask people in the same business for advice.

Before getting started in the valve business, I decided to start a pipe-fabricating business in a garage. I got an order to fabricate long lengths of pipe for an oil refinery in Texas. Pipe fabrication seemed like a great business, but I wasn't sure. I drove by a pipe-fabricating shop and stopped to speak with the owner. I explained that I was starting a pipe-fabrication business and asked his advice.

"Come back this afternoon at 1:00 p.m., and I will tell you."

Imagine asking advice from a potential competitor. I met him at the proper time. He was very honest with me as he began to explain problems and battles I would have to overcome. First the **Steam Fitter's Union** – welding codes, and a myriad of other complex encounters.

I kept thinking this is a man who frankly tells another exactly what to expect, good and bad, a person who could be a competitor. I admired his sincerity.

Try it! Walk in someday and say, "I want to start the same business you have."

Try it. The shock of learning good, truthful advice astonished me, as it will you. It seems people do like to talk about their business, their industry aches and pains, as well as the good side of things. They feel flattered that you value their advice and pour it on.

I also followed my own advice. In writing this book, I contacted another first-time writer for advice. He sure helped me and thanked me for calling him.

Years ago, I read Dale Carnegie's _How to Win Friends and Influence People_. He mentioned it was human nature for people to help others with advice. I recommend this book as part of your own notes and learning material for success. It definitely is a _must-read_. I have re-read parts often, especially when I have a confrontation with a tough customer.

I didn't get into pipe fabrication because of his advice. For example, he told me most chemical plant and refinery plant workers will not install pipe fabricated outside without a Steam-Fitters Union sticker. Imagine starting off in business with a union contract ($30,000.00). I knew valves, not pipe fabrication.

Know the product, service, or both, and then work on what is known.

Always get into a business you know. If not, one may run into a brick wall and get hurt in more ways than one.

CHAPTER 28

Partners – Outline Divorce Papers First

WHY NOT PARTNERS?

A business partner is a marriage without love. Forget about a prenuptial agreement, go further, and prepare a divorce agreement with your partner before you start the business.

Partnership – Get Divorce Papers First

Fred was the top salesman in the men's clothing department of a large department store and wanted to open up his own haberdashery. Not having enough capital to invest in his business venture, he discussed finances with his best friend, Herbie.

Herbie offered complete financial backing for Fred's venture.

Together, they found an empty storeroom, purchased $50,000 worth of inventory (in 1953, that was a large sum of money). Herbie put up all the money – that was the agreement – Fred was the knowledgeable partner that would run the company. They started the business selling men's clothing. What a partnership! It seemed as though together they possessed all ingredients for a successful business.

Not so.

Two weeks after they opened the store, Fred complained about the constant pressure, long hours, losing sleep, worrying about paying the rent, his low-profit take-home pay, loss of vacation time earned while employed at the department store, not to mention the lack of medical benefits.

Fred, not exactly the epitome of honesty during this transaction with Herbie, then admitted he never actually quit his job at the department store because he was unsure of himself, so he was trying this new business venture during his two weeks' company vacation.

"Sorry, Herbie, I just can't handle all this. Too much pressure. I need to get some sleep."

Herbie could be heard for miles as he screamed, "What the hell are you talking about? I laid out $50,000 for inventory. I helped you get into a business that could be a major success, and you're worried about losing sleep?"

Fred reminded Herbie he is a 50/50 partner, and he had better calm down and quit his screaming – partners work things out.

Poor Herbie. He had to buy Fred out. Fred got paid to quit.

This may sound like a far-fetched story, but it actually happened and continues to happen more often than not. Before forming a partnership, make a written agreement, even if it's scribbled on a piece of paper. Outline a divorce.

The need of an agreement was brought to light later in my career. I hired a manager whom I met in California. I was impressed with his sales and management experience, got carried away, and told him during the interview that if things worked out, meaning sales tripled or quadrupled, I'd eventually give him ten percent of the company.

During the second interview, he told me that he thought a lot about my offer and wanted to ask one more question.

"This ten percent of stock."

"What about it?"

"When will I get the stock?"

Immediately?

"Not exactly. The stock deal would require that you stay with the company for five years and then you would receive two percent of company stock each year."

"Why don't you give me the stock when I begin the job? Don't you think I'm worth it? Don't you have any confidence in me?" He was definitely perplexed.

"I do have confidence in you, but what if you quit six months later with ten percent of stock in my company?"

He still could not understand why I didn't trust him so I related to him the story of Fred and Herbie.

My mistake with this employee from California was that it was all verbal – no sheet of paper.

His impression was that he would eventually receive as a bonus more stock in the company. All of this was verbal. He only heard the parts of the offer he liked best. After five months, he didn't progress at all; I fired him. He sued me, claiming he moved to Pittsburgh because of my offer and was set back financially.

Let me insert this:

I did not write and confirm the terms of employment. I didn't even scribble anything regarding this position on a piece of paper, photocopying it for my files.

This little venture cost me $55,000 in lawyer fees and damages of $30,000 in 1970. Muttering and calling him every name in the book certainly didn't help as I wrote him a check. This was indeed a bitter pill to swallow. I had to swallow my pride on this one and pencil it in under my lessons-learned-the-hard-way column. Do not ever make the same mistake; your entire business may be at stake.

Verbal contracts cost money.

I never did get another partner –other than my adult children who became my only partners. This is one bit of advice my father told me – DON'T GET A PARTNER. It is better to have a half loaf of bread. One can eat the half loaf without asking permission.

It took me twice as long to get there without a partner, and I am not sorry.

I still made my mistakes, but not as costly.

One time, I contacted a venture capital source. WOW! They wanted 51% minimum ownership for a very nominal amount of money.

Another person later who was qualified and had cash was interested in becoming my partner. I sensed, somewhere along the line, he would develop an overrated opinion of his ability and then want concessions. He also would probably, in turn, feel that I had an overrated opinion of my talents, and we would clash.

I also felt I already had one partner – Uncle Sam- who is a non-working, silent partner. He costs me enough.

CHAPTER 29

What Wages to Pay Employees

Wages and what to pay employees . . . . sounds so simple, but the truth of the matter is that many battles are lost or won on this point.

Phase 1

When starting a business, pay what you can afford for clerical assistants, hire a high-school graduate with no experience. I was amazed by how many high-school students were good at shorthand and typing. They were eager to work and needed to gain experience in the business world. It does require much patience on your part, as they are young people who never worked before and find it difficult to get the first job and adapting to work hours and other self-discipline needs.

Regarding accounting services, I hired a retired accountant. He accepted less pay since he was already receiving a pension and/or social security.

Most employees I hired were young and inexperienced. It was a team of enthusiastic, incompetent people who were paid a minimum wage. All the machinists were graduates of local trade schools with no experience. Together, shop and office, we were a group of incompetents muddling through the day.

This makes life tough for the entrepreneur initially as he/she must constantly train, watch, and correct everything that is done. This is reality. You can't afford to pay good wages to competent personnel, so you spend a great deal of time supervising, training, and being patient. Working with young people is fun and keeps you young.

Here is reality, you can put off paying suppliers, rent, insurance payment – BUT NOT WAGES – payday Friday is a very lonely day – no help, you must pay!

<u>Phase 2</u>

When business gets better, hire college graduates. Hire an engineering graduate, but even then, try to keep the base pay low with a possible incentive bonus.

I got real support with the professional valve design engineer I hired. He had ability and sales aptitude. Inside of one year, he was on a bonus basis, ended up staying with me eight years. Together we made a bundle of money, and he loved the work. We made a great team.

Within a year of hiring the engineer, I hired a fresh, out-of-college accountant and a salesperson. It was at this period within my business that I could afford to hire brainpower.

Plant Manager – about fifteen years later, things were going quite well, as sales were multiplying. I needed a good plant manager for my rubber operation, since my field was a very specialized one.

I received a resume from a plant manager of a competitor. He seemed reasonably satisfied with the wages and benefits I offered him during the first interview. Three months later during the second interview, he requested another seven percent more to accept the position. I replied that I did not want to get into a bidding war with his present employer.

He said he had requested more money from his current employer after the last interview but was turned down. In fact, he was told to go take the job offered by me. This irritated him for he knew his value. He said, "I made lots of money for him."

Thus, I had my new plant *manager* who was trained and good at what he did. I got my competitor's plant manager with ten years' experience. Moral of this story: don't be cheap when the right person arrives. If that employee is making money for you . . . *PAY HIM WELL!* I am indeed lucky to have personnel that bring in the proverbial "bucks." Do not make the mistake of losing a good person to one of your competitors over a wage difference.

CHAPTER 30

Agreements

When in doubt, make an arrangement! If liability is high, make a long, thought-out agreement. When funds, large or small, are involved, make an agreement.

For example, a job-interview agreement. The candidate has impressive credentials, charm, knowledge, and professionalism. Conventional wisdom may say, "We need someone like you on our team, and eventually, you may become an owner. That is, if you bring in two million dollars' worth of business, we will pay five percent override and maybe give you stock within our company." Perhaps after a two-martini lunch, the candidate accepts your offer.

STOP RIGHT THERE!

PEOPLE HEAR WHAT THEY WANT TO HEAR. The owner said five percent override on sales, NOT five percent of the business. To repeat myself, *people hear what they want to hear, terms they like. It actually is not dishonesty on their part, as they do some dreaming too.*

Put the offer in writing. If not typed, write it all out on a sheet of paper, date it, and give the prospective employee a copy. Tell he/she to come in for another interview to review job duties and objectives.

All it takes is a sheet of paper stating salary, perks (car, clubs, etc.), ownership (if any), and terms. Tell the candidate to think about the offer and bring it back upon his return.

If it is an agreement for contract work; for example, state, "I will pour, smooth, and finish 3,000 square feet, six inches deep of concrete for $16,000. Add to this: i) work to start in ten days, and ii) completion within thirty days. Request a copy of the liability insurance policy.

A single outline-letter agreement, even handwritten, will hold up in court.

Believe me when I tell you – *people hear what they want to hear* – the terms agreed upon must have mutual understanding.

Fortunately, I took an elective course in college, "Business Law." I still remember a lesson about inferred contracts. For example, a painter shows up at your house and starts to paint your room instead of next door. You watch him, saying nothing. This is an inferred contract. YOU DID NOT STOP HIM, so now you must pay. If you were not home, then he will have the loss. WATCH OUT FOR INFERRED CONTRACTS.

PS: My secretary wishes she had made a written agreement on a house she bought with her ex. She did not – everything was verbal. She put up all the money and ended up with half when they split.

CHAPTER 31

Location – Retail Business

Are you considering a retail business?

People in business say that THE MOST IMPORTANT ASPECT OF A RETAIL BUSINESS is LOCATION, LOCATION, LOCATION.

THEREFORE, go directly to the proposed location and take an hourly count of passerbys. In fact, take two weeks to do this traffic/body count. If the body count is low, search for another location and do the same.

The next critical issue is terms of lease. Make certain after the rent is paid you have something left over. The landlord makes out, and he's off the hook by pushing you into a five-year lease with a five-year option. This is mega bucks, even at $500 a month.

When the ideal location is found, the need shifts now to finding an attorney who can draw up a favorable lease or disaster looms. A quick mental note here about a good attorney: *Ask around town in an attempt to find a professional attorney who deals in real estate as a specialty because real estate laws are a specialty and change frequently. Lawyers keep throwing new curves into leases. Don't hire an attorney that handles general cases. The only way to survive is to find that extra-special real estate attorney!* You'll be glad you did.

At this point, you must again re-look at what type of business you will start.

For example, the greeting card business.

I asked a friend, "Why did you select greeting cards as your business?"

"I am a CPA, and I feel working as a CPA is not a good, long-term future for me, so I began investigating various businesses and their profit-making futures. At first, I thought of being a beer distributor but found the profit margin low, maybe $1.00 per case. I would have to sell a lot of cases of beer at $1.00 profit to make $55,000.

"Then what?"

"I did my own market survey, spending over two months talking to people, going to various businesses for advice." This is the key phrase – asking people's advice in any given business. They will be truthful and glad to share their experiences, both good and bad, with you. I cannot stress enough the importance of advice from successful business people.

People are vain. They feel you are looking up to them because they are smart. So they pour it on, brag how good it is, and how they overcame problems. With all the good advice they give you, they end up with a handshake and GOOD LUCK, MY BOY.

If you choose the right business, at a good location, with a fair lease, you will be one of the 50% survivors your first year.

CHAPTER 32

Insurance

Are you saying you can't afford life insurance? That is a personal problem? I never carried life insurance (other than a $10,000 policy) for the first ten years I was in business.

I could not afford to pay premiums on a $200,000 life insurance policy. Product and comprehensive liability insurance for a business, however, is a <u>must</u>. Without it, a claim can end up costing, not only loss of your business, but also well into your future.

Cost of comprehensive and liability insurance is reasonable because it is based on dollar volume of business. In starting a business, your volume is generally low. Trust me when I tell you to get liability insurance.

Call an insurance agent.

Most of my inventory was carried on 90 days. The least I could do was insure my suppliers' products. They invested in me.

When starting your own business remember you can't <u>fly without insurance</u>.

CHAPTER 33

Women in Business

<u>Currently, women own twenty-eight percent of all small businesses</u>. They get into a business by inheritance or their own entrepreneurial choice.

The challenges we cover in this book to succeed are the same – overcoming the same obstacles.

One of the most interesting things we have seen happen in the late 20th century is the change in the corporate world because women have begun to take a greater part in it.

More women every year are becoming CEOs of large corporations.

Women often devote many hours of work to succeed. They can start on a small scale and build over a time period while developing various skills.

WHAT ABOUT WOMEN INHERITING A BUSINESS?

Our bank invited my wife and me to a seminar that dealt primarily with women inheriting the husband's business. Many issues were discussed. The two significant revelations were as follows:

Owners of businesses routinely go home and brag to the wife that their business is so great, it's worth two and a half to three million dollars if he sold it. He is making so much money; he's definitely going to keep it!

This is a value that, in many cases, is unrealistic, made up of 80% ego satisfaction and 20% profitability.

Upon the owner's death, the widow has difficulty accepting a low price to sell her business. After all, her husband said it was a goldmine.

The bank, therefore, is requested to find a suitable buyer at an inflated price. The bank also has difficulty in convincing the widow of another basic problem, that is, it is much easier to sell a dry-cleaning business than a specialized valve business catering to a "niche" market. How many people know valves? The number of buyers is limited.

There are many more potential owners for a dry cleaning business. It is easier to learn – no requirement for an engineering degree.

Women, in many instances, are forced into stepping in and running a business. They then are confronted with ALL the challenges and issues discussed in this book.

WOMEN EXECUTIVES WORKING FOR A SMALL BUSINESS.

I cannot end without mentioning the value of my secretary in my business. In the beginning years of my company's growth, she worked typing, answering phones, the usual secretarial duties. Several years after being hired, it was obvious she had much more ability. She applied herself, paid attention, and eventually earned the position of Vice President.

I trained her to answer technical questions about my products. Eventually, on another new product, I made her head of the division with an incentive. The new product sales grew, the company benefited, and her compensation grew as well. For twenty-two years, this "executive woman" helped my company grow.

She wanted to put her three children through college. My incentive paid off. This was her driving force.

Women employees are a vital, important part of any business. They help it to grow.

An executive who has not learned this does a grave injustice to his business and/or the firm's growth. Most women want to advance in their place of employment.

More and more women are heading major corporations.

Remember, women own 28% of all small businesses.

So Go For It. If you are a woman, go down to Home Depot and buy five sheets of ¾" plywood and start a business you have been wanting to.

CHAPTER 34

Learn to Listen

My New Jersey sales representative called me to advise me that my newly patented check valve was terrific, but it only goes to size 12", and he had a customer who required a 56" diameter check valve for storm sewers. I told him to forget it as I am having enough trouble with making a good 12" size valve that works.

Two weeks later, he called me once again asking about a 56" valve. I had to reply, No! No! No! Two weeks after that he insisted that I visit the EPA in New Jersey in order to hear what his customer had to say regarding the need for a very large-sized check valve.

When speaking with this salesman and customer, I explained that I only made this new valve product up to a 12" size and have problems producing even a 12" size. This customer insisted and wanted to know how much it would cost to design and manufacture a 56" size.

I told him $19,000, but I could not guarantee a good valve that would actually work, and I may have to build at least two prototypes.

"You got a deal!" He was quite emphatic in his statement, having a purchase order written up for two valves and telling me to, "Go to work, and I know you will make one of the two that'll work!"

This product became and is still my Number One product, which now contributes to forty percent of my total sales.

Learn to listen, sell customers what they need, not what you make easily or like to make.

You can have the best-engineered product, but if there is no use for it, you will not sell it.

Listen to the market.

Listen to the <u>needs</u> of customers.

Expand when you have to, pull back when you must, just remember, – make what the customer needs, not what you like. It's surprising how many manufacturers never learned this or forgot it.

Learning to listen is very important with employees as well. They are doing a good job day in and day out. Their mind and bodies work on your product and business, they are in a position to make or suggest changes you probably will never think of.

Just walk through your office and plant. Speak to the employees often. They are your "best friends," so to speak, and are working for you, as well as WITH you.

Listen to this. My Union Shop Steward, who I disliked (he organized my company), spoke to me one day with a bit of puzzlement. "I can't figure you out. We have a twenty-year-old relic of a forklift, which we spend two days every week fixing, and it takes two men away from production in order to fix it. Go buy a rebuilt or new forklift. You are definitely wasting your money, don't you think?"

I said what does he know. I, however, went back to my office, multiplied two full-day wage rates times four weeks. I found out that monthly payments on a new or used forklift would be less than what it cost me to repair that old forklift. Imagine a Union Shop Steward, who disliked me, and normally fought me, trying to help me.

CHAPTER 35

Payroll Services

There are numerous firms that offer payroll services. These services include issuing checks, determining deductions, year-end statements for federal income tax, social security, Medicare, local head tax, local city tax, and any other taxing authority. New burdens now in making payroll checks are allowing for loan paybacks on pension plans, deductions for garnished wages for child support, head tax, and so on.

All that is required from the employer is to call in to the payroll firm the individual's weekly hours and rates for both salaried and hourly employees.

Engage a payroll-service firm. Avoid hours that are spent balancing each of the deductions to the last penny. A typical employer may be filing forms for several surrounding city boroughs, even state taxing bodies, child support, loans on pension plans, etc.

Payroll tax deductions are sent direct by them. All this is provided for a very low fee. Many hours required for this particular phase can be utilized on more profitable business problems. It makes sense to hire a payroll service since it is relatively inexpensive. I do highly recommend it to all entering into a new business.

Headaches trying to balance to the last penny on government forms will definitely be spared.

I Repeat - The service is relatively inexpensive.

CHAPTER 36

Clarity of Thought

At times, you get to a point when you feel exactly like a juggler, keeping six or seven balls in the air at once. Hey, here come three more. Are there times when you find yourself in a state of absolute confusion? The answer is definitely yes; I was confused at times.

Now with this new "informational age" it gets much worse.

My solution, at the beginning, was to wake up at 5:00 a.m. before the wife and kids, TV, dog, and within my own solitude time, ask for CLARITY OF THOUGHT. Clarity of thought means just that.

Ask yourself exactly <u>what is the most important, pressing thing I can and need to do that day</u>.

It's like making a grocery list.

In your solitude, pick out the most important items you have to do first, and if it takes more time than you planned, that's okay. Add and take away. This does help with self-organization. It may take several weeks to get in the groove, but the brain stores information. It is the most refined computer of all, easy to use, easy to get to, and is great at storing facts. Get "on line" within yourself by asking for "clarity of thought."

Ask what is important – what should be done first.

Ask for clarity of thought from this over-taxed-information age.

Determine the inner circumference of my problem, consider all the facts as to what may be the *real* issues here.

Along with clarity of thought, get organized in the office. Your secretary hands you a pile of mail. On top of this pile is an overcharge for a rent-a-car bill. You take 45 minutes the first part of the day on this $30 charge. Three-fourths down the pile is a request for prices on your product or an order. It gets attention four hours later after a martini lunch. Go through the pile and organize it with the most important on top then start to work.

GET CLARITY OF THOUGHT.

CHAPTER 37

Role Models
(They Come in All Ages)

When you are looking to make it big at a rapid pace in the business world, look for a role model to admire, hopefully one in your contemplated venture. They are all around you and appear in all sizes, shapes, and age groups. Here is one of my role models.

For years, Nick Mitchell had a fancy fruit stand at the old Pennsylvania Railroad Station in downtown Pittsburgh, just scratching out a living because of the high rent and low traffic. He struggled for most of his life in and out of four restaurant businesses. Finally making a go of his fruit stand business at age 75.

During World War II, many of the armed forces personnel traveled by rail to various camps. They wanted fresh fruit, personally or as a gift. His business flourished.

Imagine busting your butt for seventy-five years in various ventures before making something out of your business. He was still trying at age 75 to make it.

AND HE MADE IT!

And you think you have it tough.

He amazed me. He financed his two sons through college. They inherited his money, bought real estate, and are the Yuppies of our era.

I mopped floors, helped wash walls, polished silver and brass, not to mention the errands and other things I had to do – never gave up. I can now boast of having over thirty patents. My best invention will be the next one. I own a company doing several million dollars' worth of sales – ALL BEFORE AGE 75. Nick Mitchell is my role model.

Go find a role model, or remember, a seventy-five-year-old role model, Nick Mitchell, made it.

Don't give up.

CHAPTER 38

Lawyers – Liability or an Asset?

Obtaining "good legal advice" brings to mind Diogenes, with a candle in the daylight, was "searching for an honest man." It is difficult to find a good, intelligent, knowledgeable, sincere, honest lawyer who provides excellent legal service.

The first rule, choose a knowledgeable legal consultant for the special issues, such as labor lawyers, real estate lawyers, estate planners, corporate lawyers – specialists in their field.

Rule 2, if a mistake is made, do not hesitate to change lawyers. Choose someone who will work best for the company, and remember, you can stop the clock any time you want.

We are all heartless in firing manual labor ($5.50-an-hour people) with a simple statement, "I won't be requiring your services anymore. Sorry."

Why should this be different with lawyers? I have personally hired/fired legal advisors mainly because my problem at the time was not their particular specialty or their handling of my problem at $150 an hour was not satisfactory. Every profession has incompetent people, lawyers have not cornered the market. There are smart and dumb (mediocre) ones out there, find a smart one.

I needed a labor lawyer, real estate lawyer, patent lawyer, and estate-planning lawyer to mention a few specialties. Basic rule, choose a legal specialist in the required field. Again, it is important to seek advice, locate the proper "specialist" lawyer for your particular needs. Your chances of hiring a good lawyer have now increased five hundred percent.

CHAPTER 39

Wills and More About Getting a Lawyer

WILLS.

Lawyers are important, required, and must be selected properly. My first attempt at making out a will with my attorney was in 1961. I appointed my brother-in-law, the lawyer who drew up the will, and the Bank Trust Department as executors – all three. I felt confident that I did the right thing. There were three entities handling my estate. I had three small children and no insurance.

By 1976, the sales for my company had quadrupled. My estate had grown from zero to high, apple-pie-in-the-sky, forcing me to think about rewriting my will.

I contacted another lawyer to prepare a more sophisticated will, with real inheritance tax savings. The lawyer questions, "Why do you have the bank as executor? The bank's track records aren't very good, especially with small estates. Once they have the trust, it's tough to get the bank out of it."

The bank Trust Department can lose money or break even, and I would need a lawyer to withdraw my own funds. I eliminated the Bank Trust Department as one of my executors of my estate on this first rewrite.

Four years later, the estate got even larger, and I hired another, more intelligent lawyer who drew up a more sophisticated will with bigger tax savings. He suggested that I eliminate my brother-in-law. I agreed, he could cause family problems.

It was now 1988, and on my third go around. I now was paying $175 per hour to the new attorney.

On this third rewrite, he asked me, "Why do you need an attorney as executor?"

"Well," I answered, "I thought everyone needed an attorney for their will."

"Why? Do you know that if your children begin to fight among themselves, I, as executor, cannot represent them individually or collectively?"

Another small bit of information – all an executor lawyer can say is, "That is not nice, kids, don't fight," and the lawyer executor collects five percent of our estate for the next fifteen years or until the will expires for executors of my estate.

Diogenes! I found an honest man and feel extremely fortunate.

I cannot stress enough how important it is to find a good attorney who is "honest." Change attorneys if need be. Share in the wonderful in-the-nick-of-time-learning experience. Look at the amount of money I saved (5% of my estate annually).

I am not slamming lawyers. Be like Diogenes, light your lantern and search in the daylight in all the right places for a good one.

CHAPTER 40

Hiring An Executive – Confronting S.M.O.A.

Whether it is a marketing manager, chief financial officer, production plant superintendent, or material-handling expert, I discovered that all of these executives possess what I refer to as "large-corporate mentality," the acronym S.M.O.A. defines the attitude best. Save My Own Ass principle demands no decisions be made because in the event of an error, the executive goes. The S.M.O.A. behavior dictates to the executive to call a meeting, hence a group decision, whereby no one person can be blamed.

<u>Financial Officer</u>: I hired one, which put me in dire straits. He decided to lead me into more problems – bankruptcy – enabling him to purchase the company. THIS REALLY HAPPENED. I saw through his plan before it was too late. I discovered his plan in the morning – let him go after lunch.

<u>Sales Manager</u>: Upon employing this individual, he called to my attention several months later the fact that he was a marketing man and not used to hiring, training, or firing salesmen, manufacturer representatives, or anyone. For the last twenty years at his former place of employment, he was a marketing man, had to write a business plan and submit it to the Chicago office, waiting several weeks for a reply. Among other things, he couldn't handle getting an answer from me in two minutes, so he quit. He was not a short-sleeve producer, a working sales manager.

<u>Plant Manager of metal fabricating facilities</u>: I hired this man from a very large corporation to get more valves out the door. He later advised that he was used to working with a staff of people to handle purchase of raw material, flow, order entry system, and performing all the other required functions. All he had to do was answer a few questions whenever things went wrong. If production figures were off, profits low, he would tell corporate management that it wasn't his fault the Sales Department is taking orders at a low markup. Corporate management would accept this, hence S.M.O.A.

Many large-corporate executives are out of touch with how small businesses operate.

Fat-cat executives have extremely bad habits. When they need a new job, in the interview, they do not tell you they can work in the trenches as short-sleeve managers.

Large companies pay fat salaries to executives and employees.

Large corporations are run for the benefit of the employees.

Small companies are run for the benefit of owners and hardworking employees.

Most executives are people of good intent who just developed a lot of bad habits. They are knowledgeable but not short-sleeved executives. Their desks seemingly are always cleaned, never anything piled up.

This reminds me of a statement made by the president of a conglomerate. "An executive who has a clean desk is one that is not aware of what is going on and is immune to any of the problems within the company."

NOTHING PENDING.

CHAPTER 41

Unions

I went the full route and got hit with union organizing twice. I live in a union-mentality town (Pittsburgh). Since unions are strong in this area, one must deal with them openly and honestly, abiding by their rules, cooperating with them in every way.

The first attempt to unionize was with three employees. Yes, three employees! A vote was taken announcing the formation of a union. I contacted a labor lawyer who advised me that I had to draw up a contract with the union, and the cost would be between $15,000 and $20,000 for a standard agreement.

I said, "Ridiculous, for three employees?"

I announced to the workers that I could not afford this nor would I pay this amount of money for a contract to guarantee three people's employment. A picket was threatened. Fortunately, that winter was a cold one, after two weeks of picketing, they all quit.

I would rather have given the employees more money than give this large amount of money to lawyers.

Second Round: Ten years and eleven employees later.

I was paying the going machine-shop wage, had a good employee life insurance policy, hospitalization coverage fully paid by the company, and a profit-sharing plan.

I made it a point to treat each employee quite well since I was busy, out of town calling on customers, and purchasing castings. I needed their earnest cooperation. In doing so, I must have given the shop employees the impression of being a pushover.

A union sprung up.

"Why do you need the union, I asked? You are getting a good salary and have good benefits."

"Job security," was the answer given. Such gross Pittsburgh union mentality, all this union stuff for eleven workers. Workers in their early twenties, out of trade school organized.

77

I contacted a labor attorney. He quoted $20,000 for the contract, and since I was boiling mad, and ready to fire them, the lawyer said, "Don't threaten workers with firing." Seems it was the Sherman Anti-Trust Act or something like that. The union demanded a vote.

At that time, my father was working in the shop. I asked my lawyer, "Is my dad eligible to vote? Does his vote count?"

He replied yes. I wanted to make sure since my father's ballot would be the deciding vote.

On the day ballots were cast, the union representative showed up and challenged my father's vote. His vote was invalid two weeks later. The union had won its battle.

I was mad enough to visit that attorney who said he hadn't a clue why this happened at the election.

He replied, "The case took a bad turn for the worse."

I expressed my negative remark that he take his law diploma down from the wall and wipe his you know what with it. That may not have helped my situation in any monetary form, but I did feel better after venting my boiling-point feelings on this lawyer's advice.

In his lobby, incidentally, was a monthly legal journal that discussed voting – challenges of family workers, etc. Some advise – "case took a bad hop."

The following is a brief list of other actions I learned and experienced. I was surprised to hear, for example, that lawsuits are filed against the union itself. The members of my shop actually did threaten the union business agent with a lawsuit.

One worker became so arrogant that he ran the lathe all day with no cuts, bragging about it to boot.

On another occasion, I had gotten word that one of the employees left his station, went to his car trunk, and made a marijuana sale. I questioned him in the office, and he denied the charge. He was so nasty that as I walked back to the shop, he screamed "F-you, boss man" and gave me the proverbial finger.

I was boiling mad, and I sent him home for one week with no pay.

He filed a grievance with the Union Business Agent who stated that my punishment was too severe. I stated it was my belief that I

78

should have fired him permanently, but I just sent him home for a week. The agent told me, "You can't fire on the first offense or even suspend him for a week."

"When the hell can I fire this arrogant employee? On the second or third offense? By that time, I would lose control of the whole shop."

The settlement of the grievance was two and a half days off without pay, instead of one week.

Three years later, the second round of union negotiations for a union contract.

I phoned another union lawyer and invited him to sit in on the first bargaining sessions.

At that time, I had also started a rubber manufacturing facility in North Carolina. Upon telling my new attorney about the North Carolina facility, he wanted to know about my total production capacity. I informed him after two years, it was great, and with several expansions, resulted in over capacity of production.

"Well," he said, "let me handle all the negotiations. And by the way, please do not state costs are lower in North Carolina because the union has the right to check your books. If you have over capacity, you have the right to shut down a facility, but cannot shut it down because of unprofitability. You have to prove unprofitability."

The attorney announced to the Union Representative and Shop Steward that we were closing Pittsburgh's operation, as we did not need that much production. The operation in North Carolina was enough.

The Business Agent stood up and said, "Mr. Raftis, you are a gentleman. You could have had my people on the picket line for several months and made the announcement after much suffering out there, but you told us upfront." He looked at the Shop Steward and said, "I guess that's it, boys."

The Union Agent had also been motivated, somewhat, to throw the towel in because of the thirty grievances, which eleven people filed, along with the lawsuit threat at Detroit. What an ordeal.

As explained previously, search for a sincere attorney specializing in any given field. In this particular case, I needed one for union problems.

Light your lantern in the daylight and begin to <u>seek</u> and <u>find that honest labor lawyer</u> to handle your union contract.

Can you imagine workers suing the Union? Can you imagine a labor lawyer rendering half-ass advice so he can get a substantial legal fee, $20,000, for a union contract?

Guardian angel wherefore art thou? Protect me!

Incidentally, the lawyer informed me of another company that took pictures/slides of plants closed after unionization and displayed these photos to employees. Some closings were after six months, one year, two years, etc. The slides and pictures were presented as a documentary. It I permitted legally. It does not blame unionism, just stated the results.

CHAPTER 42

Patents

I took a course in college on patents. The instructor repeated and pounded the following information:

1. Over sixty percent of the patents awarded do not earn the cost of obtaining the patent.
2. A patent mainly assures your continuance in making the product yourself that you are producing in lieu of being sued for infringement. Another person cannot stop you from producing it. This is more important than stopping someone from copying your invention.

You can regain the cost of getting a patent by deciding that you will manufacture the product. If the plan of pursuing a patent is to solicit someone to manufacture your product, forget it. You believe you can convince someone that he/she could become wealthy by manufacturing your idea, and that person should invest his money for manufacturing facilities to make you rich. It would be assuming that the person approached knows how to promote the product, which in all probability, is a niche (suitable) market. It would be assuming that this second party will accept returns, buy advertising, invest in equipment, molds, forms, inventory to make it go for you.

Think this out before you apply for a patent. Who is going to invest his/her capital to make you rich? Remember also, if someone infringes on your patent, the patent office will not protect you. They won't even write a simple letter stating that person is infringing and must cease.

You will have to sue, appear in court with, not only good evidence, but an excellent patent attorney, as well. The jury will then make a decision if it was an infringement and when the infringement must stop.

The U.S. patent office, incidentally, has sympathy of all those geniuses that lose money getting a patent. Normally, it will cost

$4,000 to apply for and prepare a patent and $2,000 to $3,000 for first action (reply) of patent office. There is another cost of $1,000 to $2,000 to receive a final award. The total is approximately $7,000 to $20,000 and unrecoverable if a patent is denied.

U.S. Patent Office, therefore, created a new program entitled "Applying for a Provisional Patent." The initial cost is $1,000 and is good for one year. One can explore the market during that time and then determine if another $7,000 or more should be spent to obtain a formal patent.

If the inventor really loves his/her's invention, then start a business, apply for a provisional patent, and go for it.

If you don't want to start your own business, keep your money – don't apply for a patent.

Do not waste time thinking someone else will invest money and time to make you rich.

CHAPTER 43

Bankers

I was completely frustrated with bankers, when I first started the business because I needed money and could not borrow it.

Basic banking policy I learned: Banks do no lend money to businesses that desperately need it to function. Banks only lend money to businesses that <u>do not</u> need it or have the ability to repay without much effort.

I had to learn all this the hard way. In fact, it has helped me now in dealing with bankers.

Second lesson: Be prepared to guarantee the loan personally. It is at this point that later I agreed with the bank. Why should the bank lend someone money who does not want to personally guarantee his own venture? Banks are in business to make a profit, not to help you out or guarantee your venture success.

What if you ask to borrow less money, something you can pay back? The bank might say the loan is so small, it isn't worth the paperwork. It's a "Catch 22" situation. Complete frustration.

How long before you personally do not have to sign up for a loan?

NEVER!

I have news for you. After being in business for forty-eight years, my wife and I still have to personally sign for a loan regardless of all my company's assets.

Banks do not want your home, business, or other assets.

Banks want their cash back along with interest.

You go home with an application for a loan. There were on-the-job conflicts and problems all day long. Finally, arriving home, there is always another crisis or problems with the children. This is reality. You forget the loan application sitting in your briefcase requiring your wife's signature. At 6:30 a.m. or 7:00 a.m. the next morning, you suddenly remember the loan application. You wake up your wife and say sign here. The wife signing takes place at 7:00 a.m.

Ask someone who has been in business whether or not he did this – woke up his wife at 7:00 a.m. and said, "Darling, sign here please." She, at this early time in the morning, would almost certainly, reply, "I can't see so you'll have to point to the signature line."

Is it on purpose or subconscious frustration that might make you forget the loan application requiring your wife's personal guarantee?

Expect also a dig – "Am I signing a divorce agreement?"

The answer lies within.

CHAPTER 44

The Restaurant Business

Why reinvent the wheel? Ask for advice.

The restaurant business is a great business. At least I thought so.

I have thirty beautiful acres on the Parkway between Pittsburgh and the airport. I envisioned a rustic-looking steakhouse with ample parking and high visibility from the Parkway. Everyone would want to dine at my five-star steakhouse. My valve business was doing well. I felt I had enough savvy to run another business.

I contacted three friends in the restaurant business for which I held very high regard. I invited them to my home for cocktails, seeking advice from them regarding my thoughts for a new business – a restaurant.

They told me the first thing I needed to do is hire myself on as a dishwasher in a restaurant for one week and see how I liked it.

"What are you talking about? I'm going into the restaurant business big time."

"That's what you think. If you get in the restaurant business, especially high class, and one day while your place is really jumping, the dishwasher gets mad and walks out. You'd better be prepared to go back and wash dishes. Because if the chef doesn't have a nice clean dish on which to place his creative endeavor, your customer leaves! One, two, three.

"Cut it out! Sounds as though you are trying to discourage me."

"What other obstacles are you going to tell me about?"

"You also better learn to cook. Chefs are all Prima Donnas. You have to cater to their whims, and there is no guarantee they will not leave for a more substantial wage, which you couldn't match."

"Let's say you have a dining room full of guests. If you know how to make soup, baked potatoes, steaks, and a few other things, and the chef walks out, you can always tell the waitresses to inform the customers you ran out of specials, and the only thing left on the menu is broiled steak or fish and baked potatoes."

"I can handle the situation because I barbecue my steaks when we have a cookout."

"Alright, go for it. By the way, are you prepared to be 180 degrees out of phase with society?"

"What are you talking about now?"

"When you enter the restaurant business, all things change, especially at night. Holidays, special occasions, birthdays, time spent with your family have to be ignored because you have to be at the restaurant. No more social or family life in the evening, and that's it. Your wife and family will carry on their social program, but you wont' be a part of it. While your family may be out having a good time, you will be working."

"You are 180 degrees out of phase with society."

"Also keep in mind this situation applies weekends and holidays, as well as vacation time. It disrupts, not only your personal life, but also the personal life of your wife and children. So, just be prepared to put yourself on a completely different schedule, never seeing your wife or family at night or when the kids come home from school."

"You've got that all wrong. I am going to run a high-class restaurant recommended by gourmet magazines. I'll have top-notch personnel."

Then they said: "name the top four restaurants in the city."

I rattled four off the bat. They asked me who owned each restaurant. I was very proud that I knew who all the owners were.

"Do you realize you knew all the owners?"

"Yes, so what?"

"This is a very important phase of the restaurant business. If you want to run a successful gourmet restaurant, you'd better be there to shake hands and meet your clientele. You like it when you walk into a restaurant and someone says, "Good evening, Mr. Raftis." Your guests hear that, and they are impressed; you're the man about town. This is all part of the big-time restaurant relationship with the owner who has made it a point to remember their names. Big-time restaurant business is built on knowing your clients' or customers' names."

"Another thing, Spiros, (well I did ask for their advice), it takes many hours to run a restaurant. If you are not going to be there, the big spenders who bring guests will not return, which brings up another point. If a customer has any particular complaint, they usually want to speak with the owner. This, in turn, gives you the opportunity to pacify him, apologizing for whatever reason, build a relationship. You will either have to offer that customer dessert or buy the drinks, or offer him another meal at a future date. You are there and can do something to keep that customer coming back to your place."

You, at least, are there to listen as they vent their dissatisfaction.

"You guys are really raking me over the coals!"

"No, we're just describing the problems. We think it's a great business, and there's a good profit if you handle everything properly. We are merely trying to advise you not to get into the restaurant business part time or without a thorough investigation."

"It's a cash business, so watch out for theft or raw steaks disappearing."

"Anything else you have to tell me?"

"One more thought. If you decide to go to a movie, and it's lousy, while walking out you say to your friend, "What a lousy movie, the acting stunk, plot was poor, and little or no emotion. However, you will return to the movie theater again."

"Yeah, I've done that."

"Well the restaurant business isn't like that. When you leave a restaurant after a bad meal, you'll swear off that place for the rest of your life, and undoubtedly, tell everyone you know about your experience and that you can cook better than that. The restaurant business is really a personal business. When people go to fine restaurants and spend money, they expect superior service, food, and drink. A combination that's hard to find these days."

I got the message. It's a universal language wherein everyone gets the message that if you decide to go into any business, including the restaurant business, you can't do it part time.

Before venturing into any business, get all the facts, search for glitches, things that would hinder profit. *Every* business requires a lot of personal attention from customers to personnel. Are the orders coming forth within a reasonable time period? Is everyone completely satisfied? Is there any way the owner (YOU) can improve things?

Managers, assistant managers, and part-time endeavors can be effective only after a business is established for many years, employees trained for many years, and you earned a well-respected reputation.

Analyze everything and anything! It is important. Take your wife/husband and children into consideration. Ask them what they think. This is important. You might miss your children growing up. This is just a "beware" sign for your own good.

That's why I also suggest being <u>careful in selecting the type of business you want to enter</u>. AND ASK FOR ADVICE.

Restaurants require tough hours away from family.

CHAPTER 45

Yellow Belly

I jump all over the place with incidents as they come to mind. They all have a bearing.

When I was working as a sales representative on my first job, I was riding with another salesman from Wheeling, West Virginia, to Pittsburgh, Pennsylvania. During the trip, he told me about how his incompetent, alcoholic, inept boss carried on. He would get drunk and embarrass him professionally. He raved, "My boss is plain stupid."

Forty minutes after listening to his whining, I had a chance finally to say something. "You have to be even more stupid than your boss! After all, he doesn't work for *you*. It is the other way around, you work for him. What's your problem? Don't you have enough guts to just up and quit? Go into your own <u>damn manufacturer-rep business</u>. Ever think of that? You certainly know the business and are smart enough."

I told him what an excellent salesman he was. Since he held an engineering degree, he could detail in depth to customers all the advantages of any technical product. He already had a proven sales record.

As a grand finale in my pitch to give him some gumption, I said, "If they took a knife and cut your belly, yellow puss would come out. You're afraid to start a business." Horrendous as these words sound, I felt it was necessary to get my point across to a man that needed a push – no a shove – in the right direction. Sometimes that is what a person requires. His reaction was one of extreme anger, as he verbally exploded, telling me off in no uncertain words.

He said, "You SOB, I went through the African campaign, Anza, Italy; Germany. Eighty percent of my platoon was wiped out. My mother's Hail Mary's saved me, and you call me yellowbelly."

Fortunately, I saved my advice to when I was outside my home. I slammed the car door closed and got out.

Incidentally --

He took my advice, and within one year, was in business for himself --

And was a big success.

In my opinion, do not wait for someone to call you gutless or a yellowbelly.

In fact, most people would not dare tell you something like that. This little episode tells you a bit about myself   When it comes to helping others, I definitely got guts – I tell them off! I hate to hear complaints. Blaming others for their misfortunes.

My advice, stop at Home Depot, buy five sheets of plywood, and GO FOR IT!

CHAPTER 46

The Silent Partner

Headed for a tough meeting or situation coming up? Say a prayer and ask God to come in with you as a silent partner. During the meeting when the going gets tough, remember the silent partner is with you, and say in thought, *they don't know they cannot win because I have my silent partner helping me.* It works, believe me. I have used it several times in my lifetime in extremely difficult situations.

As Jesus said, bring your burdens unto to me to resolve.

I have talked to several executives and shared this experience with them. Several related that they also went into tough meetings with the same "silent partner" and came out victorious.

God does help and so do prayers.

Try it.

CHAPTER 47

A Business Disaster – A Fire

I had a disastrous fire in 1968 that leveled my plant. I was in Philadelphia at the time. One of my employees, therefore, relayed details of the event. He started telling me every move worked against me.

The fire truck, first of all, stalled outside the fire station for twenty minutes because of engine problems. When it finally arrived at the burning plant, it took another fifteen minutes to connect the hose to the hydrant because they hydrant was frozen shut. Finally, after thirty-five minutes, water was reaching the burning building – a bit too late. It was an inferno.

Also by that time, the 440-volt power line going into the plant got red hot from the fire and fell down, cutting the fire hose in half. It took another ten to fifteen minutes to hook up another hose. Can you believe all this? As fate would have it, my employee also informed me the wind then suddenly picked up, fanning the fire at an uncontrollable rate, generating forceful flames that spread at a rapid pace. Nothing remained untouched by the fury of that fire. It brought down everything with crashing, blackened disintegration. He said it was unbelievable how many things went wrong.

AMORI ORA! (Desolation Time).

The next day, my insurance agent came and assessed the situation. He invited me to lunch. Prior to going to a restaurant for lunch, I asked him to stop in front of a church, as I wanted to spend a moment at the church to light a candle.

My prayer to St. Mary was, "In case you have anything else in mind, "I've had enough."

MI XIPOTERA (things could be worse).

I just couldn't take it anymore. I had worked hard, and within an hour, everything was gone, poofed away by Mother Nature's wrath. How do I handle this without falling apart?

I admit to drinking my lunch that day – three or four vodkas. They failed to relax me. This event was pure hell. There seemed to be no relief or answers.

Many business associates came around that week giving me encouraging words, hopefully, to help me through this situation. They truly were real friends, advising me not to worry about a thing, and perhaps it was for the best because I could now construct a new building and lay out plans for the manufacturing plant the way I really wanted it rather than the hodge-podge plant I had. I could also buy new machinery, get rid of bad inventory. The insurance would pay for everything.

I, however, could only feel my total loss.

My insurance wasn't that big.

I was wiped out.

A total fire with your business being burned to the ground is *traumatic.* Money isn't the question. Defeat is in there with the loss.

Others said, "Why don't you sell out now rather than rebuild?" Your customer following is worth money."

How do you sell a burnt-down business?

More advice was forthcoming from well-meaning friends, bankers, and insurance people.

I went to visit my mother, who had a third-grade education in Greece, but being truly wise and knowing her son's every feeling, she sensed that I was nursing self-pity, fear, and defeat.

"Son, I want to tell you an old adage in Greece. Aboard merchant ships, the captain is generally drunk most of the time. The mates run the ship. However, when there is a big *Furtona* (violent storm), and the possibility that the vessel may sink, they call that drunken, sea-faring captain to take the helm and reveal his *axia* (value) as a captain. Translated, this means he will now, at this possibly disastrous moment, show his worthiness.

I was wiped out to the tune of three-quarters of a million dollars – most of which I owed. I felt depressed, as well as defeated. My mother, I thought, was telling me FAIRYTALES.

On my way home, however, I began to think about her story. What was she really trying to tell me? Simply this – if you really are a capable captain, you will overcome this disaster, and if you aren't a capable captain commanding your business, it will sink.

That's all there is to it.

Her advice started giving me self-determination more than all the opinions previously received from bankers, insurance people, and lawyers.

Hell yes, I said. I'm a capable captain and can stay afloat. I will not go down with my ship. I have ability, determination.

Thanks to my mother, I once again had the will to go onward and upward, to rebuild.

Command your own vessel like a true captain during a storm and say, "AXIOS, I am CAPABLE."

CHAPTER 48

Why Are You Living?

When the pressure seemed to become heavier than I could bear, I began visiting psychics, fortunetellers, spooks, and took up reading metaphysical books, one of those books being written by Edgar Cayce and his dissertation about reincarnation still stays fresh within my mind. He claims a person's mission on earth is catharsis of the soul and believes that if one's soul is not clean when death happens, the person will then be reincarnated, receiving another chance.

I don't believe in reincarnation; however, if he were right, I'd best be good because who in the hell wants to go through all this again.

Man is a total person of all his experiences and knowledge. If you grew up in a ghetto or a non-intellectual environment, your outlook is totally controlled by these particular surroundings. It is difficult to perceive oneself. Therefore, either move as a turtle, very slow, or react as an entrapped deer, and quickly jump out of it.

My father used to say, "Then Xeris Yati Sis (You don't know why you are alive)." I kept ignoring him, figuring it was just an old-time Greek saying. One morning, I asked my father for the answer to, "Why am I living?"

"To grow up, my son, and become an honest person, a good worker, get married, have many children."

I replied in a sarcastic manner, "What if I never get married?"

"I'm certain your intended mate will come forth at the right time. It is meant to be, you will see," he replied.

She did enter my life. My wife is a blessing and truly a gift from God.

I read Onasis' life, Nikos Kazantzakis, and Elias Kazan all from Greek parents. They stated in their books the same challenges from their parents – Then Xeris Yati Sis."

At age forty, I read the in-depth reply – Kazantzakis' *Return to Greco*. It took reading not only this book, but also all his books to get answers.

Nikos Kazantzakis in <u>*Return to Greco*</u> states the soul lives on forever. His book is worth reading.

For example, in <u>*Zorba the Greek*</u>, Zorba asks the professor, "What's it all about?"

The professor replies, "We are amoebae feeding on a leaf. The leaf is the earth. The tree is the universe. All the amoebae are busy eating the leaf (earth). The lucky ones are those that lift their heads and look out at the immensity of it all and wonder."

CHAPTER 49

General Mills

I cannot finish this book without relating one real ridiculous episode that happened.

I was in business for approximately nine months when receiving a phone call from the Vice President of Engineering of General Mills. He was interested in my pinch valve, stating it was ideal for handling flour and sugar. There were no pockets for food decay.

He stated, "I would like to come and visit you because we like your product."

By that time, my office had expanded a little, plywood being replaced by a cement block, two-person office. However, there still remained a dirt floor, old desk, typewriter, and four folding chairs. I had started construction of my cement block, 20-feet-by-30-feet (see photo) "plant." It would be embarrassing to receive any client, much less a bigwig from General Mills. I, therefore, informed him I would be in Chicago, and it was a short trip from Chicago to Minneapolis.

"No, no. I'm going to the Food Show in New York with my chief draftsman. I will be flying in our company's jet, so I will come to your office."

I shook a bit before I continued. "When you get to Pittsburgh, call me, and I will pick you up at the airport because the plant is located on a hilly, unpaved, dirt road and may be difficult for you to find."

Ten days later that appointment was confirmed.

I asked my wife to come to work, play secretary, and type some sort of fake letter. She replied, "I can't come over there, you have no toilets!"

I told her, "try to visualize what I go through on a daily basis, just picture eight months of annihilation."

She said, "You really must need me" and agreed to come to work.

The road to my facilities was muddy and full of ruts. It was raining that day as we were waiting for the phone to ring.

Around 10:30 a.m., there was a knock on the door. Two immaculately dressed men, complete with mud on their shoes and the cuff of their pants, came halfway into the door. It was the vice president and his draftsman.

I said, "You should have called me from the airport."

"Well, we thought since you were the President of the company, you would be busy. We hailed a cab, but it couldn't make it up the hill, so we had to hoof it part of the way."

"Come in and sit down." I reached for the folding chairs. They stared at the dirt floor and my wife, who was nervously typing a letter that said nothing.

We discussed features of the valve. They were both in agreement that it was a good valve for food service – no pocket for food decay – simple to operate.

"May we see your production facility?"

I stated that no one was working; it was hunting season and the men were all off. I had just begun building the cement block plant ---- there was no glass in the windowpanes.

"We want to see it anyway."

We entered the plant. At that moment, the rain had turned to a light snow, which was blowing through the plant (and I use the term "plant" loosely) and there was some snow buildup on the small junkyard lathe.

This is the truth.

"Mr. Raftis, you have no glass in the windows."

I replied, "We Pennsylvanians are a hardy bunch." What could I say? That was the first thing that popped in my mind.

"Son, if you don't get some glass in these windows soon, you are going to freeze your ass off!" The vice president almost cracked a smile. The draftsman choose to keep his mouth shout.

With that remark, I realized just how ridiculous the situation really was and began to stutter. "Let's g-g-g-go b-b-b-back to the o-f-f-fice." It was either nerves, or I was shivering from dampness and cold. Who knows?

Obviously, they had noticed the stupid set-up, but we talked about valves, but not for too long. They were chilled from head to toe, but at least they had trench coats on for a little protection against the weather.

I started to stutter again, "L-l-lets g-g-g-get b-b-b-back to the airport." I just couldn't talk. Yes, they agreed.

I drove them back to the airport, not much was said. To lighten the atmosphere, I did say, "I recently moved from another facility." Suddenly an ugly thought ran through my mind – they now must imagine how decrepit the other facility must have been from the looks of the new facility. My best bet at this time was to shut up the rest of the drive to the airport.

They said I had the kind of valve that would handle flour, sugar, and not plug and had no pockets for food decay.

Talk about life's trying-not-ready-yet moments.

A small postscript at this point: They bought a few valves, but no matter how good the valve was for their particular need, I was in no position to furnish them in the many sizes they required, nor was I equipped to provide quantity. Much to my dismay, I knew I could never win over their confidence again.

Win some, lose some.

This is not only in life, but also in business.

I kept going though and you will also!!!

CHAPTER 50

Tranquilizers

One day I went to work and developed the shakes while drinking my coffee. I went straight to the doctor's office wherein he advised me that my blood pressure, pulse, and heart rate were all normal.

"Why do I have the shakes?"

"You're tense, worked up."

"I'm going to give you a prescription. Take these pills for one week. They will help calm you down.

"Are they tranquilizers?"

"No. Nothing but strong aspirin."

When I got home and showed them to my wife, she advised me that they were indeed tranquilizers.

"That's it. I'm going to Puerto Rico for a week or two, and if I don't calm down, I'm selling the business. I'll be damned if the business requires that I take these or any other pills in order to run it."

My wife was quite surprised with my reaction, and that I actually booked the ticket the next day to Puerto Rico for ten days.

Anastasia is a lovely, understanding wife, and at that time, we had three growing children, but a very small insurance policy. My family would need food and shelter for at least the next twenty years.

I came to terms with myself in Puerto Rico as my thoughts became more relaxed and sincere.

What came to mind was the philosophy of President Truman's – if you can't handle the heat, get out of the kitchen.

I made a pact with myself – no tranquilizers – no narcotics – maybe a little booze. I chose to utilize my brainpower instead. After my two-week vacation, I returned relaxed, found direction, started drinking, reviewed my goals, and looked forward to the business' future with great expectation for not only myself, but also my family.

Tranquilizers are not the answer. I NEVER take them as they represent a false hope and only work temporarily. The problem you have has to be faced head on, only one way, the RIGHT way. Cleanse your mind, and fix it with thoughts of correcting whatever is wrong.

There are therapists you can speak with, if necessary, but talk, cry, yell, scream, only <u>do not take tranquilizers</u>.

Business requires a brain running wide open at all times. Get a good night's rest. Do not let the business overpower the belief in yourself, have more than enough confidence so that whatever goes wrong <u>will</u> and <u>can</u> be fixed. When you think you're at the end of your rope, tie a knot at the end, and hang on. Keep up your strength; take some time off to give yourself a new perspective and goal.

Stay cool and remember your health always comes first. Without it, you are unable to function properly, much less run your own business.

If tranquilizers are needed – sell out – walk away. Your health comes first.

Why am I tell you all this? Start a business, and you'll know why.

CHAPTER 51

Goals and Cutting the Mustard

Set realistic goals.

My particular goals at the start, were:

1. To become independent.
2. To be awarded for the fruits of my efforts in direct proportion to my ability.
3. Not getting fired after building up a territory.
4. To set a goal of $20,000 to $25,000 annual income (this was back in 1953). Something attainable not a multi-millionaire-pipe dream.

Set reasonable goals that are attainable.

After you reach your initial goal, you can set new goals. They also must be reasonable.

Confidence in one's self is definitely important.

NEW GOALS

1. Can I cut the mustard?
2. Increase sales fifteen percent per year.

Money is not always the motivation; it is merely a fringe benefit.

Determine what motivation is best for you.

The challenge counts.

Can you cut the mustard? You bet!

Part III

<u>The Value</u>

This next section covers different phases and confrontations in family succession.

Author with wife

BETTER DAYS ARRIVED

George Raftis

Chris Raftis

Cynthia Raftis

Author standing next to 90" diameter storm water valve

Patents on display
Red Valve Co. Lobby

First Trade Show Exhibit
Also made in house of plywood

Left: Original Red Valve plant site in 1953,
was an abandoned strip mine site.
Right: Red Valve Co. Rubber Manufacturing
Plant in North Carolina

CHAPTER 52

Family Succession

DO NOT REINVENT THE WHEEL.

The best way to succeed in "Family Succession Planning" is to go to the phonebook, library, or the Internet and get help early in this process.

There are many Small Business Associations that have seminars on "Family Succession."

In writing on this particular subject, the reader audience is as diverse as are the owner's personal needs that it is difficult to suggest a particular path.

Begin by reading and listening. I did with extreme absorption. Every chapter I read on the subject is imbedded in my mind. A few axioms:

First Basic Axiom: During the first year, eighty percent of all businesses fail. Of the survivors, twenty-five percent more fail within five years. The next failure is thirty-five years later when the founder runs out of steam.

Thirty-five years later is definitely not the time to begin thinking and teaching your sons and daughters how to run the business.

Second Basic Axiom: You cannot give advice from your grave nor can they be expected to ask questions from an Ouija Board or at a séance!

Other statements proliferate, "Nobody can do it like dad," and "how about training us while you are alive, dad!"

Most people I spoke with had problems with their dad not letting go of the reigns.

If your father is a doctor, chances are you will be guided in that direction, serving within the medical field.

I know a couple who are both lawyers. They had a daughter who became a paralegal and a son who was totally convinced (possibly brainwashed) that there was no other field available in life but the law. Both children work within their family's firm.

Even when there is a professional Naval, Air Force, Army, Marine, and Coast Guard officer within the home, chances are one or more children in that family will choose the same branch of service. It's inevitable. Your surroundings help you choose direction, but you may turn your head towards another direction.

Not all offsprings want to go into their parents' business and prefer taking their own time to find themselves, to discover what they want to do or become in life. Sometimes this process of finding oneself never ends.

No matter what, it is important that the profession/business you are involved with be introduced to your children at an early age so they can become familiar with every aspect of the business, making their own decision later on if they are forced to run your business or decide it is their best option.

Keep in mind there are many consultants and firms who deal in family successions. If you want to introduce your children to the family business at a much later stage in their lives with the hopes they can handle it, do so with care.

Go to a consultant first and then take your sons/daughters on the second visit. As an overview, I have seen better success using this method of help as opposed to contacting the consultant after you've proceeded to make a mess of everything.

Do not reinvent the wheel!

CHAPTER 53

Is Your Succession Planning Easy

Winery businesses in Europe pass through, not only one generation, but as many as four and five generations! Most of the time, their succession passes on to the eldest son.

There are many businesses in the United States run by fourth or fifth generation --- both big and small.

This is old-world thinking, old-world family patience, and oldest-son philosophy generally practiced within European and Middle East countries.

You live in America. The family wealth and business is generally divided more often among all the members of the family.

With some companies, the transition is simple. For others, it becomes traumatic in nature.

THE EASIEST TRANSITION IS FOR THOSE WHO HAVE JUST ONE HEIR. THEY ARE LUCKY.

A cop-out is to bring in an outside manager, particularly for the small businesses, not letting the sons/daughters run the company and grow with the business, especially if they want to run your business. An outside manager will put an end to their hope.

CHAPTER 54

Siblings Day-to-Day Confrontations

Encouragement is the Name of the Game.

All young people need encouragement, enabling them to develop brainpower and management skills. Every progressive step each of my sons took received an avid "attaboy" from me. I looked for things to simply "attaboy" them.

When my sons entered the business, I would compliment them in many ways. "You saved us money." "Great decision." "Liked your letter." "You handled that meeting like a pro." "Son, he thought he had you cornered." "I would have done it the same way."

If they asked about a problem, I would analyze the difficulty of the problem and then relate a solution letting them know that I was confronted with the same situation.

Starting early with information before you run out of steam is the most fruitful approach. Day-to-day incidents, business confrontations, and money policies are a few of the many business problems they should take part in.

Rather than solve problems alone, bring in a second-generation member, and have them listen and contribute advice or suggestions – regarding compensation, establish a salary base for owner and family members, and establish incentive bonuses based on increase in sales or bottom-line profits.

Explain the business is not a refrigerator, meaning that every time he or she hungers for more money, a new TV, or boat, they cannot open the refrigerator door to satisfy this urge. It does not work. Take out only what one earns and establish a salary. Work out a compensation based on sales or profit, but definitely include an incentive.

There must be money left in the business to pay the bills, supplies, wages, insurance, utilities, and unforeseen expenses.

Compensation plans with incentives create control. Teach this to your adult children.

When it comes to buying machinery, it should be discussed with sons/daughters. For example, a CNC machine can turn out a valve body completely machined in twenty minutes. CNC machines cost $750,000.

I sit down with my sons and discussed the pros and cons. For example, calculate hourly wages required turning out one hundred valve parts, add to this the vacation and holiday pay, workmen's compensation, company's share of social security payment, life insurance (even a $2,000 policy), and hospitalization costs.

Tell them no need to do an extensive feasibility study. This study in large corporations dictates the CNC must operate a minimum of two shifts with consideration given for a 200% payback.

Family-owned businesses make a decision that afternoon, with the shortcut immediate, quick-cost calculations. You want to enjoy profitability and the sales advantage of faster production as outlined above.

Inventory turnover is important. Explain why.

NEW PRODUCTS: Another second-generation discussion. With large corporations, prototypes cannot be built before a market survey and a feasibility study. This study can cost $25,000. They question is, even if the new product works, what is the market?

Small family-owned businesses can build prototypes of $2,000, test it, and offer it to a few customers. Feasibility study money went into building a "rough" prototype.

We introduce at least one new product every year. New markets open up with new products, and sales increase.

Other straightforward answers to business problems are required every day.

The problems are more meaningful if they are part of a son/daughter's daily confrontation.

Problems do not have the same impact when reading about them – confrontations do.

YOU CANNOT GIVE INSTRUCTIONS FROM THE GRAVE!

You'd better give them before that time comes.

Start early while you are still young, full of energy, and have patience.

I, personally, know four owners of manufacturing businesses who never had their sons in the business.

"Why?" I asked.

"Because my son is just plain dumb."

Another person answered, "Because my son just doesn't have what it takes."

They all asked how I did it. My answer? It began many years ago with the "Attaboys."

Actually, I don't see how anyone's child can be "dumb" unless he happens to have a superhero type of father who performed brainwashing tactics on his son, actually making him believe he was dumb. No "attaboys" here, just the usual father constantly nagging his sons, making statements like, "What the hell is wrong with you?"

This is pure unadulterated verbal abuse by the parent. That child certainly knew he could never be as smart as his father. (Basically, he probably *was* a lot smarter, had he been given the chance to prove it.)

If you have a problem, reread Chapter 5, Fear of Failure. Rename it. "I put encouragement in my sons and daughters."

I wonder where the mothers are allowing this sort of thing to happen under the same roof. Many fathers, and mothers in some cases, are simply egotists – domineering people – not even realizing they have pushed their sons or daughters over the edge, placing them a in a state of mind considerably below average. Most of these adult children end up having no self-respect and develop an attitude of NO HOPE.

Help your sons and daughters; let them take part in household events, as well as in the family business. They need to feel participation, to feel needed, respected. They require your attention. When they have a question, answer it as best as you can. Just let them participate someway in whatever the family has to offer.

I read another book, <u>*Domineering Father*</u>. It stated that a high percentage of leaders are "Domineering People." That's how they got there. They can't stop when they get home. Don't dominate your wife and kids.

I am glad I read this book. I had some domineering ways myself and decided I better "BACK OFF."

I decided a "Domineering Father" is wicked. I never realized how destructive this is to young people. I thought scoldings were normal!

CHAPTER 55

Decisions

One of the first of many matters I discussed with each son and daughter was related to making decisions.

I told them employees would come and ask them to make decisions within one week after they start work. Yes! One week!

Most employees do not want the responsibility. Consequently, tell your offspring the employees will push decisions on them.

I gave my children authority to make $1,000 decisions immediately for the first three months.

I also handed them the following schedule:

After three months:	$ 20,000 decisions
After one year:	$ 50,000 decisions
After two years:	$100,000 decisions
After three years:	$500,000 decisions

After that, if you think your decision can bankrupt the company, then talk to me or at least phone and discuss.

Other than getting them immediately involved in the business, you are also inferring to them they are smart enough to make decisions.

Most questions are minor problems.

Son, daughter – BE LEADERS, SHOW THE WAY!!!!

CHAPTER 56

Parental Influence at Home

Everything on earth, everything in the cosmos, and everything astral seems to touch and affect you, serving to help you learn, grow, evolve, improve, and achieve your goals.

Therefore, you cannot expect a child born in Calcutta, Bangladesh, or Sarajevo to have the same brains and outlook as a child born to an American family, even if they are born within the exact precise moment in time. We are dealing with energies that flow and influence, not with the fixed and immutable.

Consider this aspect with your offspring – your daily routine, the casual conversations in your home – what influence do they have on your offspring? The experience they've had and listening to you talking about various subjects to others definitely influences their thoughts.

Certainly, compared with small talk in Calcutta and rural, backwards areas, there is no comparison.

Point out that if he/she wants to be self-employed, America is the land of opportunity. There are articles in local newspapers and magazines that write about self-made individuals. Cut these out and give them to our son(s)/daughter(s).

Single parents have an even greater task in building up their own self-confidence, much less the self-confidence of their child since they are usually already taxed to their limit with work and other obligations.

Take advantage and build on this!

Encourage your offspring. If you don't get him/her in the business, encourage his/her career, be it teacher, hairdresser, airline stewardess, circus clown, whatever strikes his/her fancy.

Chapter 57

Succession Planning –
Why the High-Failure Rate
After Thirty-five Years

The reason for high-failure rate of businesses after thirty-five years is lack of planning for the future. The founder of a business, even at age sixty-five, is convinced nobody is as smart as he or can run the company as well, particularly an offspring or relative.

He forgets the next generation was born with a computer in their lap and the information explosion.

I repeat, statistics state over eighty percent of ALL businesses fail the first year! Fifty percent of the survivors fail within five years. Thirty-five years later, the failure rate again zooms. Why?

Simply, because the owner ran out of steam, joined country clubs, played golf, went swimming, took trips to Europe, and even got involved in politics. He found himself purchasing luxurious vehicles – Mercedes, Jaguars, Lexus, or Cadillacs. Let's not forget the expensive Condo living. I plead guilty to all of the above.

The owner (father) says, "Well I saw to it and hired a good manager." He forgot the manager was as old as he was and generally possessed an even less amount of steam and drive! The owner believes his son/daughter will eventually learn from the manager's instructions. Not so!

Most founders actually never take time to think the problem out. Therefore, there is no second-generation coaching and results in the high-failure rate.

This is not what I did. I got them interested before I ran out of steam.

CHAPTER 58

Silver Spoon In His Mouth

I read somewhere that it takes the founder a lifetime to hit one million dollars in sales, and the second generation goes to ten or twenty million easily.

My philosophy was let *them* build it up; let *them* take the pressures. Youth can handle it. The founder? He's liable to die of a coronary!

I made sales calls with my sons. Spent time in the shop and office answering questions regarding product manufacturing, discussed improvements, innovations, and dealing together with them with banks, lawyers, CPAs, and customers.

I heard the expression you can't give instructions from the grave VERY EARLY.

My philosophy was that I wanted to enjoy what I had earned.

Let them all work now for future growth! Do I still work? Of course! I get involved with projects I like. The one I enjoy the most – developing new products.

I hold thirty-two patents and even now working on new ones. That keeps me out of their hair and the day-to-day problems of the company.

Occasionally, the boys don't exactly like the way I run my projects. I simply hang in there and listen to them. They have a chance to observe my fumbling and perhaps will avoid doing the same thing.

I discussed with them the obstacles all second generations must deal with.

NUMBER ONE OBSTACLE:

Son of Boss (SOB). He has it made. First thing he has to psychologically fight is his peers. Fellow workers don't say too much, but they certainly think it.

"His sons sure have it made!"

Baloney is what I say.

Both sons bust their ass. They have more responsibility than kids their age deserves. Dad says, go ahead, son, keep up the good work. You can do it!

So tell your sons/daughters in the business:

Overlook the SOB title.

You will do it well.

I'm proud of you.

You are really good.

Don't let fellow workers intimidate you.

Expect subtle remarks.

CHAPTER 59

Hey, George Made a Mistake

George made a somewhat serious mistake. He knew it; I knew it. I didn't cuss him out or call him a dummy. Mistakes, they occur almost everyday, in every place of business or at home. We all make them. I don't care who you are or what you do; you will make mistakes.

Nobody noticed my mistakes, and if they did, they kept their mouths shut.

When George made his first serious mistake, I said nothing that day or the next. I didn't speak about if for three weeks.

After three weeks, I said, "By the way, do you remember such and such goof up three weeks ago?"

George replied, "I have been worried sick wondering when you would bring the subject up and yell at me."

"The easiest thing I could have done was to yell and curse when it happened, and it would have been over right then and there."

"I guess that's right."

"This way, you have been thinking about your mistake for three weeks, and hopefully, you have learned something and have also come to the conclusion that you lost our money, not my money. Remember, I made mistakes running the business.

No one yelled at me. I wasn't being soft.

No one was looking over my shoulder.

I should extend to you the same courtesy.

CHAPTER 60

Intimidation – Malaka

Do not intimidate your offspring.

Better to <u>light</u> a <u>candle than curse</u> the darkness.

When I was growing up in our parish, there were three altar boys buddies who had successful fathers – one father being an attorney. He made it because the ethnic trade trusted him. I don't believe he knew very much about the law, let alone encouraging his children.

Every time this attorney's son did something, even a little stupid, his father called him a "Malaka." The Greek word Malaka translates into "one who makes it soft." In other words, he called his son a JAG OFF.

This boy was so intimidated that he was, still is, and always will be a failure – a Malaka. Never a word of encouragement from his father, i.e., "You did good, son." Even when he brought home an "A" on his report card, the old man's reproach would be "Oh, so you finally got one. It's about time."

The other altar boy's father had a restaurant. His old man stayed on his back like you wouldn't believe. He tolerated a steady diet of Malaka.

"Why can't you be smart like Spiros, the sexton's son?" There was no end to the verbal, mental beatings that boy had to take day in and day out.

"Spiros works five hours, goes to school, and receives A's." If only he knew how hard I had to work for a B or C.

His father had him working four hours a night in the restaurant.

His son told me, "Listen, I live in a neighborhood where all the kids have money. I have to work for good grades – study harder. I should be studying, not jerking sodas! My father forces me to work. You, Spiros, work because you have to, whereas, I don't have to. I need the four hours to study. My old man is nothing but a tyrant. He hates my guts."

Result: He could not run his father's restaurant even when he was forty years old.

The third altar boy had a dad who also thought his son's middle name was Malaka. He dropped out of college in six months, put a brick through a department store window, and performed many similar acts, costing his father money. His father had him hospitalized when he smashed the window, claiming he had a nervous breakdown to avoid jail.

Many successful people are domineering. That's how they got where they are in the first place. Unfortunately, they carry this attitude home with them. This attribute of dominance is normal and natural to them; they do not realize what tyrants they are. The wife and children definitely suffer under these conditions. An extremely dominating man generally takes it out, not only on his child, but his wife as well.

I read a book about this subject, *Effects of Domineering Parents*.

Glad I did. I observed myself as being domineering. It helped me tone down. I started letting them come up for air!

Back off man. And dad, don't you be a "Malaka!"

CHAPTER 61

Invite the Second Generation
to Run Your Business

How do you get your children to want to get into the business?

It really begins with building up their self-confidence as they are growing up.

Ask them to give the family business a try. Tell them it's all going to be theirs eventually. Tell them to learn how to run it and make money for the rest of their lives.

Fortunately, my sons and daughter wanted to join the company. I guess because they heard mostly positive comments from me through the years about the business (or real bragging).

They discovered they could get a company car. They did not have to pay car insurance, gas, and other perks. They realized all the perks afforded for being your own boss, and that more perks would be forthcoming. They liked this. Point this out.

Do whatever it takes!

Just remember, however, entering your family business may be what YOU desire them to do, not necessarily what your sons/ daughters really want. At least earnestly make the offer if they have a desire and have not planned a specific career.

I thank God for my children. They earnestly wanted to join the firm.

My business associates tell me, "Your two sons and daughter really love the business. They're dedicated, workaholics, positive thinkers, and have good marketing skills."

I reply, they are the reason our company has tripled sales since they joined the firm.

CHAPTER 62

The SOBs (Sons of the Boss)

Youth can handle it.

My philosophy is "let them take the pressures." In all probability, youth can handle what the founder can't.

My philosophy and yours should be enjoy what you've earned.

Start early in order that they have a chance to watch your own fumbling through life and business. Perhaps they can avoid the same mistakes. Admit to your heirs that you've made a few mistakes during your lifetime.

"By the way, boys, your mother and I are fed up with this business. It's time to collect my salary and travel."

You grew up with small business problems and learned how to cope with all that stuff. They have serious big-business problems. Things have changed. Everything is different now.

So, cut some slack to your children.

There definitely are bigger problems now such as new environmental laws, the Internet, higher insurance rates, increased government regulations, fuel costs increases, postage rates, computer glitches, etc. The next generation has weightier decisions. Train them at least with answers to the simple problems you had.

The person I feel sorry for is the SOB whose dad gave him the responsibility but not the confidence. Who tells him, and continues to tell him everyday of his life, that he doesn't know what he's doing. What is tougher for a young SOB than to be called a dumb ass every day by his father, or even occasionally, while employees are thinking he has a big, shiny silver spoon in his mouth!

It happens, that's why I am repeating myself.

It happens. This is the reason sons and daughters walk away from a business.

College doesn't offer a course on "How to Raise Your Children 101."

You're on your own.

CHAPTER 63

The Old Man's Idiot Mistakes

People and business associates say, "You have made it son! You inherited from your father a profitable business, along with a legacy you must live up to!"

BULLSHIT!

He left stupid work policies, investment in some bad real estate, outdated inventory, bad leases, outdated equipment, useless inventory. I could go on and on. Dad, however, was "Straight-Shooter Honest" (just a little stupid).

I say BRAVO to the second generation that overcomes this inheritance ovation and must work in today's environment.

I told my friend that on my 50th anniversary, I thanked God that I am living in America.

I thanked my dad for working hard, sacrificing many thing, spending hours talking to me about what people are like – partners, etc. I attribute much of my success to his conversations. Even though my father did not have a business, he knew human nature and relations, and those were the best lessons I learned growing up.

I HAD AN OBLIGATION TO PASS IT ON, AND I DID.

I have a daughter, Cynthia. She took over my real estate holdings. I erected three new office buildings. She was so smart; she built the fourth at a lower cost per square foot than my other buildings. Her building looked better.

She learned human nature and relations well. This now is the most important part of her work --- dealing with tenants.

You can do it, Cynthia. She did it!

I would be a failure in life if I merely enjoyed all the goodies in life and didn't make a greater effort than my dad to develop enthusiasm, management skills, challenges, and goals for my sons and daughter.

My father invested his labor, sacrifices, and his entire life to make me who I am today. I, and you, and I repeat, therefore, have an even bigger obligation to do the same for my sons and daughter.

CHAPTER 64

Dad, Let Go of the Reins!

I joined a Family Succession Group.

There are many such organizations that are worth involvement. These seminars are free or have a minimal charge.

These group meetings are to exchange thoughts and policies on succession problems and solutions. I served on a panel at one of these seminars.

Many participants complained in that session that their <u>fathers would not let go </u>of his control of the business. Sons/daughters work hard to help make it profitable, but <u>dad refuses to let go</u> of the reigns (some even after five or ten years).

I didn't have that problem because I trained my heirs to be much smarter than I, not to become Nerds! I consider it a tribute to me if my sons and daughter are better than me.

A friend of mine told me his sons are so smart that they represent the only competitors in the world that could wipe him out. He didn't say that out of fear, but rather for pride on the job he did training his sons.

I know a man on the other end who owns a large string of fast-food stores in the Pittsburgh area. He refuses to give up the reins. When he goes to the Caribbean on vacation, he is phoning instructions back. There is no justification or trust here, particularly with his own flesh and blood, his sons.

When he dies, he definitely <u>cannot secure a phone</u> extension <u>from</u> his <u>grave</u> or use his cell phone. Cell phones are not developed that good yet.

CHAPTER 65

Moral Support

Of all the previous advice, the most important statement to your son(s) or daughter(s) should be:

You are doing a great job!

This is why I am again repeating this very important attitude throughout the book. Build self-confidence in them. You tell them:

You did a much better job than I could have.

Here are some of my lines for appreciation and support I gave to my children:

You bought castings cheaper, you sub-contracted work to several machine shops to manufacture some of our parts cheaper at a savings. Bravo!

You didn't sacrifice quality for profit.

You bought labor-saving manufacturing equipment and metal-fabricating equipment at attractive prices.

The air conditioner for the building is a superior design and has lower fuel costs.

George, Chris, and Cynthia did a better job than me!

I truly believe this.

CHAPTER 66

More Than One Heir

The easiest scenario for Succession Planning IS WHEN YOU HAVE ONLY ONE HEIR.

Two or more heirs – now here is a large can of worms. If one is a girl, the problems magnify even worse.

More than one heir – two sons, one daughter – any combination you can think of.

What's the problem? Why should the daughter have equal rights or any rights to shares?

The problem is that all men and women are NOT created equal!

Common Sibling Confrontation: "She's a girl, what does she know?" Even though many women take over companies and are successful and smarter.

"I'm smarter than my brothers, why should I be left out?"

You will hear comments such as, "This brother is too domineering," "he is quicker at numbers but dumb on decisions," "she can handle people better," or "she is sarcastic." Each offspring with their own set of "missiles."

IT CAN AND DOES GET NASTY.

I met a girl at a succession seminar who said to me, "They are all bastards. I hate them – my father, the lawyers, and my own brother. "Why?" I asked. They threw me out of the company for the stupid reason that I am a girl, and women don't need the money as much as a man with a family. That's why they threw me out! The succession attorney even supported their move to bring peace."

I met a man who threw his own wife out of a family succession plan. She worked in the business for years! What a son of a bitch he was. He hired a manager.

Many a company hire consultants who specialize in family succession conflicts.

The only good advice I heard was when confronted by a decision about siblings and you decide to turn over the keys and the running of the company, you should tell them:

"You're not getting this company for free. You must agree to accept this gift with the following commitment – that you will always work together as a team. Love one another."

Three sticks of wood can be broken easily individually, but bind them together, and they are tougher to break.

Appointing a board of director may be the answer.

One man told me he had his sons and their cousins write a report on how they would run the company, what plans to build the company they visualized. They all read each other's report – the leader was obvious. This worked for them.

There are founders that appoint an outsider to run the business. In one case, the founder appointed an attorney with instructions to let the two sons and daughter take over when the attorney felt they were qualified. Two of the sons have MBAs in Business. Six years later, after the owner died, the attorney still liked his salary and perks so he voices an opinion that they are not yet prepared to run the company. He would not even hire them for any important position.

In the next section are guidelines and in the Appendix are organizations and firms that can and will help.

They will help siblings learn the importance of communicating as equals.

They will address the personnel issues of strategic and succession planning.

They will have siblings appreciate the differences in people and blend the strong points in each into a solid team.

Part IV
A Consultant's Brief Guideline on Succession Planning

by

John Ward and Craig Aronoff

A Consultant's Brief Guideline on Succession Planning

Succession is a lifelong process, not an event. Mr. Spiros Raftis understood this as he so eloquently told us throughout these sections that he wanted to have his family in his business, and he wanted to ensure that HE did not stay too long in control at the helm. This process of successful succession is more understood today than in the past, and best practices are presented at programs all over the world such as those at the Family Enterprise Center at the University of Pittsburgh.

John Ward and Craig Aronoff have long been thought of as the leaders in the family business field. As founders of the Family Business Consulting Group, they have consulted with many of the <u>leading families around the globe</u> as they move through the generations and have written many books on the subject. Once a founder understands that he has a family in business in his hands, he can start to plan what is next. Ward and Aronoff lay out their strategies for success in their series of books on the subject called *Family Business Leadership Series*. The steps to succession planning are as follows:

1. Establish a Family Participation Policy.

Some families welcome all members into the firm; other families have policies that state entry is dependent upon jobs available that match member skills. Policies should outline spouse participation and rules for salaries, bonuses, and use of company assets such as planes, cars, memberships, etc. If you are planning to give stock to family members not in the business, develop governance models for passive shareholders, as they become a source of dissention if not given a voice or understanding of what is happening in the business.

2. Provide Excellent Work Experiences to All Without Identifying Successor too Early.

Prepare family members for entering the business by assisting in the completion of their education, and if possible, outside work experience. Oftentimes, it is easier if the first boss is not dad or mom. Once they enter the firm, develop a job description with annual goals attached. Mentor the member as they learn all aspects of their job and <u>provide positive encouragement</u>, which cannot be overstated. It is critical to their sense of accomplishment, as well as their self-esteem.

3. Commit to Family Business Continuity.

Mr. Raftis made the decision early to keep the family in the business and not to bring in outside management. This is not always feasible due to age or preparation gaps. The most important criteria here is that the decision is made and communicated. This puts the family, employees, and other stakeholders on notice that this founder has a long-term perspective and is planning for another generation of the family to be in control. This also alleviates any game playing by the controlling generation that keeps everyone in the dark as to what's next or what the future holds. A family mission statement or creed is a good way to firmly let the world know your plans.

4. Design a Leadership Development Plan.

Every generation of a family business is unique and faces its own set of challenges. Sibling partnership stages tend to be more intense and volatile than any other. As a <u>result of growing up in the same household, the level of intimacy and emotionality is higher. Siblings carry into the business all those memories and opinions of each other</u> that they have held since childhood. Because each sibling may own a substantial minority in the company, a family business can be put in jeopardy when one sibling is angry, disenchanted, or unproductive and isn't functioning as part of the team. Siblings need to acknowledge that they hear, think, decide, and communicate differently. <u>They also need to develop skills to deal with these differences – communication, listening, empathy, and appreciation for differences.</u> They also need to develop policies for input and interacting with each other's spouses. This can be in the form of family meetings or family councils, but should not be ignored. Pillow talk can be hurtful if not dealt with and understood upfront. Plan for each of their roles and watch carefully as the leader skills emerge that the company will require taking it into the future. Then start to formulate your idea of your successor.

5. Have an Active Board of Directors.

An active board of directors includes experienced non-family business leaders and individuals who are not tied financially to your firm such as your attorney or accountant. All corporate boards serve legal functions, approving changes to bylaws or articles of incorporation, approving mergers and acquisitions, declaring dividends, and so on. But generally, board functions derive from five key roles: i) ensuring effective governance, ii) monitoring and improving business policy and strategy, iii) providing advice and counsel to management, iv) overseeing succession planning, and v) supporting family shareholders. <u>If you are not ready for a full board, consider beginning with an advisory board</u> or by adding several non-family members to your existing board.

6. *Clarify Business Strategic Plan.*

Most entrepreneurs hate formal planning. They have built successful businesses without it. They favor action over talking. They live in the present convinced uncertainty makes it impossible to predict and plan for the future. Experience shows that planning is critical for long-term success in the family-held business that intends to remain that way. The business strategic plan and the family succession plan are interdependent and must move down a path in sync, not in isolation. The process of planning forces owners, mangers, and all members of the family to make timely decisions and also to keep their finger on the pulse of their family, business, and the global changes that surround us daily.

7. *Fund Parents Personal Financial Security.*

Experience has shown that until the current generation feels that they are financially secure, it is difficult for them to transition out of the business. The business has provided them a lifestyle which they are comfortable in and that they intend to continue. They do not want to be held hostage by their children when it comes to their financial matters, and they are not going to be put into a situation where they have to ask for money. As with any retiree, they need to have their financial instruments in place that provide the income for their *lifestyles* and are not dependent upon the swings of the business.

8. *Identify Successors or Succession Selection Process.*

While succession is a lifelong process, most of the work of preparing for the transfer of authority and control can be done in five to fifteen years. Most owners begin thinking bout succession in earnest at bout 45-50 years of age with plans to retire at about sixty-five. Typically, their children would be twenty-five to thirty with their formal education and outside work experience behind them. Beginning at this stage allows the twenty-five years needed to make a choice among multiple candidates. It allows time to develop and groom potential successors, to give them a chance to demonstrate their abilities and to pull together a family executive committee or family succession task force to help. By the time succession actually takes place, the process will be understood and the likelihood of conflict reduced. Once a successor has been chosen, five years is usually enough to permit training and testing of the heir apparent and to execute a smooth leadership transition.

9. Complete Transfer of Ownership control.

This last step is, of course, the most important and often the hardest to do. You have set the path, picked a successor, and now you must transition to the next part of your life. This is the time that you need to let your carefully chosen and prepared successor find their own managerial voice. You get to do all the things that you never had the time for because of the demands of the family business. Devoting time to activities that will be at least as creative and exciting as those you are leaving behind is critical to your satisfaction with the rest of your life. Your reward will be in setting back and watching the next generation taking your family business into the future and preparing it for transition to your grandchildren and great-grandchildren.

Excerpted from the Family Business Leadership Series by Craig E. Aronoff, PhD. and John L. Ward, PhD. Visit www.efamilybusiness. com.

RESOURCE LIST

Part V

Start-up, Accounting, and Finance Guide

by

Mr. Joe Myers

This Is Heavy

Now that you are ready to take the chance of going into business for yourself, you face re-cutting time. You now have to deal with the business of the business. You now have to ask yourself how do I mange this creation; this idea. An entire industry has grown up on the very concept of business people not being able to mange their own business. This is the "Management Consultant" industry. These people generally command high rates per hour to advise you on how to manage your business. Your accountant or lawyer may actually be filling this role for you.

This chapter is designed to present some basic start-up problems and ideas. This chapter explains the basic organization structures available to you.

It is worth noting that before you decide on the type of enterprise you wish to operate, you need to understand your motivation in this whole process. For example, do you wish to pay as little tax as possible? Or are you looking to take your company public? This long-term outlook is important on how you organize and how to run your business. For example, it has been my experience that major corporations tend to be more concerned with increasing earnings, which improve the overall stock value of the company, while individuals and family-owned businesses tend to be more motivated by tax savings.

As a start-up, you generally do not have anyone with big earnings per share. But you do have to show your banker earnings. Therefore, at the start, you need capital and a paycheck; you do not need accolades. In other words, it's okay to show a loss "if it makes sense tax wise." Of course, you will need to explain your loss to the bank or other creditors, but that may be better than paying taxes with your much-needed capital.

First things first.

Provide for yourself.

Most consultants and bankers would suggest a financial plan. Banks like that sort of thing when you apply for a loan. You need to meet your plan, or the bank will lose confidence in your company – more on that later. So when you put the plan together, make sure you provide for yourself. Factor in a salary. You need to feed your family, and you need to live.

Factor in the taxes.

There are three or for basic forms of organizations: a sole proprietorship, a partnership, and a corporation. Under current tax laws, if you incorporated, you can be a "C" corporation or a Sub-Chapter "S" corporation. Of course, if you're in the clergy or a charitable organization, you can be a not-for-profit organization. This is a bit misunderstood; the name is not for profit – not non-profit. Just a quick note here, many not-for-profit organizations make huge profits; they just do not pay taxes. Many of the executives take large salaries and are touted as fine, upstanding citizens. Their organization simply does not pay tax; the Reverend Jesse Jackson comes to mind instantly. If your organization did not have to pay taxes, how large of a salary could or would you take? Of course, the salary too is taxable, but think of how much more capital is available to pay salaries because you do not have to pay taxes. The top tax rate for individuals is 39.6% and is effective for taxable income in excess of $283,150 in 1999 and $288,350 in 2000 regardless of filing status. For married persons filing individually, the tope rate starts at $141,575 and $144,175 in 1999 and 2000 respectively. The top tax rate for a corporation is 35% on taxable income over ten million dollars. Don't forget about the state; they also get a cut.

When choosing an operating structure, keep in mind the tax savings are actually in the state taxes and not from the federal income tax. For example, in the state of Pennsylvania, the corporate tax rate is 10.5% while the individual rate is a flat 2.8%. In Pennsylvania, it makes sense to be a Sub-Chapter "S" corporation to reduce the total tax rate to the individual shareholders. We will discuss the different organizations later.

Let's talk a bit about the major failure for a business. The fatal error that small business people make, from which they rarely recover from, is not charging enough for their product or service. This tends to snowball into a financing problem because in order to make up for the poor pricing, they finance the business with the government's money. They do not either remit state sales tax or state and federal payroll taxes. I cannot over emphasize this enough.

The reality of the matter is simple when it comes to remittance of withholding taxes or sales taxes, "IT IS NOT OUR MONEY!" Payroll taxes and withholding taxes are your employees' money, and the employer's portion is tax like any other tax, it has to be paid. In fact, this is your employees' money as well. The government simply has a duty to protect the rights of the citizens of the country, and they do it quite well.

They get real mad when you do not pay the tax. Not even bankruptcy can save you from paying taxes. The officers of the corporation cannot hide behind the corporate veil. The government will go after them individually. Sales taxes are the property of the state and now counties. They use this to fund schools and professional sports stadiums. They get upset if they do not get their money. They may work with you by letting you pay off the unpaid taxes as if it is a loan, but don't miss a payment. Not a good habit to get into financing your business by using the government's money. Late penalty payments are steep as well. Not at loan-shark rates, but steep, plus interest.

Simply, its not your money, collect it, and send it to the government. Charge enough for your product and service or do not get greedy (some people are not reputable and will steal these monies) if you expect o be in business for the long term.

This brings up the issue of overall finances. You need a plan. A simple plan, but a plan nonetheless.

YOU NEED SOME IDEA OF HOW FAR YOU CAN GO BEFORE YOU RUN OUT OF MONEY.

How much you may need to borrow at the bank or have available at the bank, such as a line of credit. Point to note, if you think you need $30,000, double it and get $60,000. There is always a pitfall you do not anticipate. If the bank won't finance you, then what's left? You could use credit card debt. This is tricky and requires a lot of careful monitoring. In this day and age of competition among banks for credit cards, you probably get three to four applications a week, at introductory offers. The nice thing about credit cards is that debt is unsecured. The bad thing about credit cards is that the interest rate is high, and you eventually have to pay a great deal more.

Build a slush fund. The principals of wealth apply to every organization. You've got to have savings for a rainy day. Putting away ten percent or some amount of cash is a good idea. At first you will think how will I ever pay the bills, meet payroll, etc. This you plan for as well.

A plan – a financial plan. Keep it simple: list out the expenses you expect to incur, including your salary. List out the revenue you expect to generate. Subtract the two. This is expected net income. This is as simple as it gets. Do this for twelve, eighteen, and twenty-four months. Adjust your plan as the facts and circumstances change, but keep the plan alive. Look for the downtrend, and adjust your business strategy. By the way, if you do not understand something, ask. Never be afraid to ask. If you do not understand your plan, do not execute it. This would be failure eminent. Only if you understand it can you manage and control it. Your professionals, lawyers, and accountants love extravagance in planning and ideas in research; they charge by the hour. They are the experts, but they can go overboard with ideas and strategies that, on the surface, will make you a lot of money, save a lot of taxes, yet it never materializes. They will send you a nice letter, which you won't understand, and probably won't implement. Keep things simple at first and second and third. It is the only way to keep control.

Manage your financial information, don't fear it. It usually is what it is. The accountants generally do not just make stuff up. They occasionally make mistakes; that's another reason to keep your finances simple and understandable, so you can spot mistakes in the numbers before you make an ill-advised decision.

Determine early on in your business what the key indicators are. They are sometimes financial in nature and sometimes operation in nature. For example, inventory turnover, days outstanding to collect receivables, total orders booked in a day, total amount shipped, GROSS PROFIT MARGIN, number of inquiries, cash in the bank, etc. Learn your indicators, and keep a close eye on them.

Your employees: "here today, gone tomorrow."

In my opinion, there are two types of employees to hire – doers and thinkers.

I suggest that in the beginning, you will need doers. The only person who has any vision and is capable of thought is you. You are hiring people to do things for you so you can go out and do the things that make money. Some of the tasks you need to accomplish are technical, such as accounting or engineering. Nonetheless, for the most part, they are repetitive tasks and need done everyday. The fact that they are repetitive is evidenced by the fact that most accounting and engineering systems are computerized.

If you hire thinkers, be prepared to change our vision or change your employee.

Sole Proprietor. This is when you simply own the business. You file your taxes on Form 1040, Schedule C. You are entitled to all the expenses incurred to generate income like any of the other forms of organization. You pay tax on the net income at the individual t ax rates. You also are subject to self-employment tax or social security if the net income of the business is greater than $400.00. That rate is 13.0% double the rate for an individual, but net the same taxes paid to the government if you were an employee with earned income. One half of the self-employment tax is deductible, just like the employer's portion of social security is deductible to the business. The advantage of this type of organization is that it is simple. There is no formal filing with the state to register the entity; the entity can cease just as easily as it started. The disadvantage is that all of your personal assets are at risk in the event of liability. You have no legal entity to hide behind. If you plan on being in business for a long time, this is not the entity to use.

Partnerships. This is a sole proprietorship for two or more people. However, administratively it is a little more complex. If you form a partnership, you will need to decide how the profit and loss is to be split between you and your partner(s). You can split the profit and loss any way you and your partner(s) agree to do so. The partnership files a partnership return – U.S. Form 1065. No tax is due with the partnership return; this is what the professionals refer to as an information return. Your share of the profit or loss is reported to you on a form called a K-1. Every partner receives a K-1. This form is in essence the W-2 for the partners. The partners report the income or loss on their individual tax rate. This is interesting in that the partners could all be in different marginal tax brackets and, therefore, pay more or less taxes than their partners. The accountants like this because it presents the opportunities to minimize taxes by shifting income. However, better to get the income and pay the tax. Now keep in mind that just because there is income does not necessarily mean there is any cash. The cash could be tied up in accounts receivable or inventory or in notes receivable that one of your partners has. Remember income does not always produce cash, more on this subject later.

The legality of a partnership in its base form makes every partner liable for every action of every partner. One partner's actins can put every partner's personal asset at risk to cover the liabilities for the partnership. Before you form this type of organization, you better be sure of whom you are in business with. One partner stiffing another partner is not uncommon. Even the accounting firms were at risk at one time from this type of entity. This is why I suppose they are picky about who becomes a partner. However, with everything else, the system tries to make things equitable, so LIMITED PARTNERSHIP and LIMIT LIABILITY CORPORATIONS were written into the law. Both of these entities operate essentially the same as a partnership but attempt to limit the liability of each partner shareholder to their interest/investment in the company and company's assets. There are no formal fittings with the state to form most partnerships.

Every time a partner leaves, for whatever reasons, including death, technically the partnership ceases and a new one is formed. Liquidation of a partnership is tricky because of the basis each partner has. This is strictly a tax concept to determine gain or loss and also the deductibility of losses. Basis essentially is what you put into the business, plus profits, less withdraws, less losses. This is akin to your cost in a stock.

If you decide to form a partnership, get a formal partnership agreement. This is a document that explains the division of the partnership, establishes the partnership, and explains the reason and purpose of the partnership. This document explains the deal in the event there is ever a misunderstanding of he original agreement. Formalizing agreements is never a bad thing. If your business associate does not want to put your agreement into writing, run as fast as you can because a big, mean dog is chasing you, and you will get bit.

The final major entity is a Corporation. A corporation is like a partnership and is a separate legal entity. Shareholders or stockholders own a corporation. When you form a corporation as a business, you are not only a stockholder, but if you work in the business, you are also an employee like every other employee. Well not like every other employee because I am sure you will take full advantage of your ownership and vote yourself to the presidency of the corporation. You must chair the board of directors. And since you make all the decisions, you are probably the chief operating officer. And since you will make the financial decisions, you may as well be the chief financial officer, as well. Someone has to control this unruly bunch of executives, so as a shareholder and director, you better hire a Chief Executive Officer. Probably someone you can trust, someone with your vision and foresight, someone you can communicate with quickly and will follow the board's direction, someone like you.

You see, a corporation can be more complex. First you have to register with the state. You have to have a charter; a set of by-laws to govern the operation, a slate of officers to run the corporation, and meetings to discuss the course the corporation is on. These minutes of the meeting need to be recoded for all concerned to review. Interesting that on an IRS audit, one of the first things the IRS asks for in a corporation is the minutes of its meetings, boards of directors, shareholders, and any special purpose meetings held. Much is documented in the minutes, much is not. In a small start-up company, it is a good habit to have minutes. It shows that there is the form of the corporation. The IR likes that. They think you are playing the game properly.

Taxes. A Corporation is a separate legal entity and required to pay taxes. The low-end bracket is 15%. This does not receive much press because there is no glamour in reporting small company income. This bracket s from $0 to $25,000. From a planning standpoint, if you have a lot of other income that pushes your personal income into a higher bracket and you start a business that generates income, by not incorporation, you may be paying more taxes on the business profits than necessary. Every situation is different, but do not just set up an entity without knowing all the exposures. Of course the government wanted to give the little guy a break, so they created the Sub Chapter S corporation concept. This, in simple terms, is a big corporation that receives all the legal benefits of being a partnership. That is, the income is passed through to the shareholders in proportion to their ownership and reported on their personal income tax returns. Not all states recognize S corporations for all industries, so it gets a little bit complex. Beyond the scope here. The key is that you get the benefit of corporation legal protection and taxed at the individual rate. But you will remember this may not be a big deal since the federal individual rates are actually higher in top brackets than the corporate rates. But do not forget about the states. They often cause a situation where the combined federal and state rate. So you've got to plan a little and understand your situation.

It is not likely that you will be involved in a professional corporation, so I am going to discuss it at this point.

Limited and partnerships are typically associated with real estate investing and syndication. The way they work is that a general partner is established who acts as the manager. The limited partners are generally investors. The concept of a limited partner is that the partner's liability is limited to his investment and the assets of the partnerships.

146

Budgeting.

As I mentioned earlier, you need a budget. Now do not misunderstand that this has to be a complicated process. A budget is a guide. It is a living document and can really help the ship when things get off course.

The underlying principal of a budget is to list out everything you know about the business you are getting into. Most business fail because of financial reasons in the first year.

So after you've listed all of our assumptions about your business, which includes how much you are going to make in total or gross revenue. This goes at the top of the page. Next, start listing out the expense items. These are salaries, rent, utilities, cost of materials or products you are going to sell, office supplies, and son on. The difference between the gross revenue and the expenses is the net income. Expenditures, such as equipment, are capital in nature. That means it is going to last more than a year. These are not expenses but rather assets. They are recorded on the balance sheet. The balance sheet is a listing of what you own and what you owe. The difference is what you are worth, called net worth, or net equity. Net worth is the measure of true wealth. Positive net worth is good, negative net worth is bad.

The equipment you purchased and recorded as an asset is presumed to have a useful life. As such, you should reduce the value of the equipment over its useful life. This is known as depreciation and will ultimately become an expense of the business. No free rides. Everything becomes an expense. However, how much to depreciate every hear has been a subject of accountant's debates for years. The accountants have developed many methods to calculate the amount of deprecation expense. In the old days, this was an area of much disagreement with the IRS. You see, the more depreciation expense in a year, the lower the income. So in 1980, the federal government statutorily determined useful lives of assets and the method to use. Since 1980, Congress has changed the system several times in an attempt to raise taxes. The most notable are the changes to real estate, which has gone from depreciation over twenty years to thirty years to 18.5 year to 39.5 years. What a half a year? Who knows, but it must have generated enough tax revenues to keep the life from being forty years, but not enough to be thirty-none years. It also gives the accounts an additional calculation to make.

Conclusion

In starting a business, there is no single bit of advice that will ensure you success. As you have read in these many pages, there are many obstacles, unexpected confrontations, and challenges. Hopefully, this practical guide will help you overcome a few of them.

I did not anticipate these challenges and confrontations. This is why I wrote this book. Most of the people who read this book say to me, "Spiros, I went through all of this – lawyers, bankers, waking the wife at 6:30 a.m. to sign loan papers. Like you, I was driven; that's why I made it."

As I look back at my lifetime endeavors, all I can truly conclude is:

God Bless America!

Because - - - -

In America, you have a better chance of success. I have met many retired entrepreneurs while in Florida (my winter residence). These are native-born Americans and immigrants who made it from scratch in diverse types of businesses. They struggles and sacrificed. Universally, they *all* say *God Bless America!*

They are the majority of wealthy people now in America. People that inherited wealth are now in the minority.

In England, France, India, Japan, and Greece, the struggle is many times more difficult, almost next to impossible. Bureaucracy stymies their growth.

Americans are the most innovative people on earth! Americans look for and want improvements. Their success is attributed also to the fact that they bring a product to market one or two years earlier than competitors overseas – Americans excelling in marketing.

My company, for example, can attribute its ongoing growth, not only to new product development, but also to an ongoing, first-in marketing ability.

If you can't afford a large budget immediately for marketing and advertising, do this as soon as possible. Start with a limited budget right away.

Develop the ability to *PULL YOURSELF OUT OF THE BUSINESS* and look at it objectively. Where are you going? Is it smart? Is it stupid? Does this new agreement or commitment represent a good investment or jeopardize you? Can you lose it all?

My company, for example, replies, "No Quote" if the job is really large, and profit margin is low.

Be a practical person. Join trade organizations because members help each other.

Don't reinvent the wheel.

Clarity of thought – right decisions will make you successful and rich.

Puling yourself out of the business and looking at it objectively will guide you. Practice it – you will get good at it. Oftentimes on a plane trip, I would look down and say, "What am I really doing down there?"

Keep your heirs in mind. Don't be so wrapped up in one thing or another and neglect encouragement to them.

Make "attaboy" or "attagirl" part of your vocabulary. They are automatically looking up to you for advice and information.

My hours were 6:00 a.m. to 5:00 p.m., Monday through Friday, half a day on Saturday. That drained me enough. I had a life to live, a wife and children, the new notion of "Quality Time."

Don't forget to ease off. Stop and smell the roses.

Getting them into our business has many benefits. You will run out of steam. Spend some of the "gold" you've made for yourself. Enjoy your life!

Your children may be smarter than you, as in my case. They grew up with a computer in their lap!

Almost anything can be figured out with the expertise of computer Internet connections. Give them credit.

Good luck – make every decision with care and knowledge. Pray for clarity of thought. You, too, can be a success.

Appendix

WEBSITE AND RESOURCE LIST FOR FAMILY SUCCESSION
1. FAMILY BUSINESS CONSULTING GROUP
In addition to the Family Business Leadership Series discussed above, there are numerous other books as well as a monthly newsletter on topics of interest. Leading speakers are avail be to your organization on family business issues as well as private consultants. Visit www.efamilybusiness.com or call 1-800-551-0633.

2. FAMILY FILM INSTITUTE
Numerous books and articles are available as well as listings of all university-based educational programs and seminars. Visit www.ffil.org.

3. CENTER FOR CREATIVE LEADERSHIP
Offers a wide range of training programs, seminars, and workshops at four locations nationwide. Areas include leadership and management development affecting change, creativity, and organizational skills, working with others, and promoting teamwork. Visit www.ccl.org or call 919-545-2810.

OTHER RESOURCE LIST
UNIVERSITY OF PITTSBURGH
The Family Enterprise Center at the University of Pittsburgh Katz Graduate School of Business provides educational programs for the family in business. Other activities include assistance with formulating board of directors, and peer advisory groups. Contact Mrs. Ann Dugan, University of Pittsburgh, First Floor, Posver Hall, Pittsburgh, PA 15260 (412-648-1544) for details.

Mr. Craig E. Aronoff, Ph.D.
The Family Business Consulting Group
1220-B Kennestone Circle
Marietta, GA 30061

Mr. John Ward, Ph.D.
1111 Forest Avenue
Evanston, IL 60202

Mr. Jim Kwaiser
Challenges, Inc.
911 Aztec Train
Mercer, PA 16137
1-800-273-8307

Mr. Robert Williams, Esq.
Williams Coulson
15th Floor
1500 Two Chatham Center
Pittsburgh, PA 15219
412-454-0222

Suggestive Reading
How to Win Friends and People by Dale Carnegie
The World is Flat by Thomas L. Friedman

About the author

    Spiros G. Raftis was born and raised in Pittsburgh, Pennsylvania. He graduated from the University of Pittsburgh in Metallurgical Engineering.

    Spiros married Anastasia, and they have two sons George and Chris, and a daughter, Cynthia. All are involved in the Red Valve Company located in Carnegie, Pennsylvania. His current endeavor is designing new-style valves for environmental applications. He currently owns over thirty patents.

* * * * * * * * * *

    As an overview, or as I look back, I have come to realize that my biggest assets were my self-confidence and determination.

    You will need both of these to succeed.

Spiros G. Raftis

Printed in the United States
72276LV00006B/7